JOHN TAYLOR ARMS

PLATES OF PERFECT BEAUTY

JENNIFER SAVILLE

Honolulu Academy of Arts

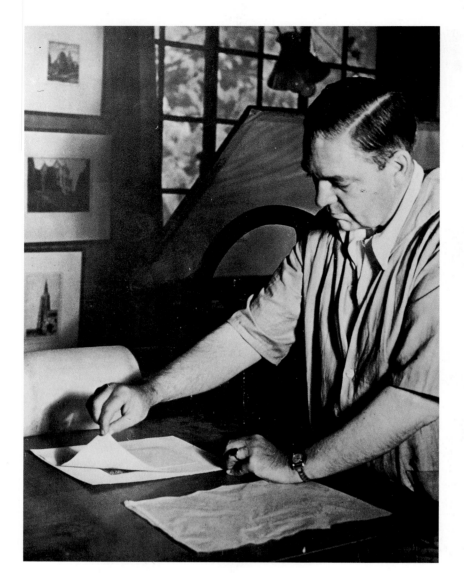

Front Cover
The Gates of the City, 1922
Etching, aquatint printed
in color
8⅞ x 8½ in. (22.5 x 21.6 cm)
Purchase, C. Montague
Cooke, Jr. Fund, 1987 (19,947)

Back Cover
A Roof in Thiers, 1921
Etching on green paper
6⅜ x 3⅛ in. (16.2 x 7.9 cm)
Gift of Richard H. and
Helen T. Hagemeyer, 1989
(20,635)

Title page
La Bella Venezia (detail), 1930
Etching printed in brown ink
7¼ x 16½ in. (18.4 x 41.9 cm)
Gift of Richard H. and
Helen T. Hagemeyer, 1990
(20,853)

Left
John Taylor Arms pulling an
impression in his Fairfield,
Connecticut, studio, 1940.
From the Print Room Clipping
File, Print Collection, Miriam
and Ira D. Wallach Division
of Art, Prints and Photographs,
New York Public Library, Astor,
Lenox and Tilden Foundations.

ISBN 0-937426-33-4
Library of Congress 96-75566

Designer: Roger L. Morrison
Project Managers/Editors: Tom Burkett, Legacy Communications, Inc.
W. Donald Brown, Honolulu Academy of Arts
Produced by Legacy Communications, Inc., Ojai, CA

Printed on acid-free paper in Korea

This publication is supported, in part, by the National Endowment for the Arts,
a federal agency, and the Andrew W. Mellon Foundation.

John Taylor Arms

Table of Contents

Foreword

The Honolulu Academy of Arts houses a collection of approximately 12,000 Western works on paper, roughly 10,000 being prints. The museum's founder, Anna Rice Cooke, included several hundred prints in her initial 1927 gift, and subsequent donors have made significant additions which have strengthened and enriched our holdings. One of the single largest donations was made by Eliza Lefferts and Charles Montague Cooke, Jr., between 1927 and into the 1950s, a gift which included an important cross section of American printmakers' work. Among them were approximately twenty works by John Taylor Arms.

In 1988, some three decades later, Helen T. and Richard H. Hagemeyer made their first donation of Arms prints, the total number growing to 170 by 1993. Their significant donation as well as funding for conservation and preservation of the collection enabled the Academy to mount an important exhibition of Arms work in 1993. This publication serves to document the collection further, making this important resource known and accessible beyond Hawaii's shores.

I am extremely grateful to the Hagemeyers as well as the National Endowment for the Arts for their support and encouragement of this project. Jennifer Saville, the Academy's curator of Western art, has acknowledged and thanked the many other individuals and organizations who have made significant contributions to this effort. To all of them I would like to add my sincere thanks.

Ms. Saville was untiring in her efforts to mount an exhibition of value and distinction and to author a publication of scholarly importance. In both cases she clearly succeeded in achieving her goal. She is owed our sincere thanks and appreciation for a job well done.

Additional aspects of our Western graphic arts collection will be presented and published in the future, dependent on time and funding. Many Academy friends have together created a rich resource for study and enjoyment in the years ahead, one which is of special importance to this island state.

George R. Ellis
Director

Acknowledgments

The writing and publication of *John Taylor Arms: Plates of Perfect Beauty*, a catalogue of the collection of prints and drawings by one of the premier printmakers in the United States in the collection of the Honolulu Academy of Arts, represents a confluence of circumstances joining donors, research, and funding support. The Eliza Lefferts and Charles Montague Cooke, Jr., Collection, donated to the Academy in 1927 and built on by the Cookes into the early 1950s, is an important resource for the study of American etching of the first half of this century. Their gift of almost twenty prints by Arms provided a firm footing for the continued growth of the Academy's holdings of his work, which received an extraordinary boost with the donation of 170 prints by Helen T. and Richard H. Hagemeyer during the years 1988 to 1993. The Academy is deeply appreciative of such support. The assistance of the National Endowment for the Arts has been instrumental in bringing this publication to fruition. It would not have been possible without its commitment to the project.

The research and detail-specific cataloguing that underlies this publication results from the cumulative efforts of a number of Academy volunteers and staff members, as well as the cooperation of several libraries and archives. The assistance of the staff of the Prints Division of the New York Public Library and the Prints and Photographs Division of the Library of Congress was enormously helpful as was the cooperation of Adrienne Aluzzo in the Midwest Regional Center of the Archives of American Art. Her prompt attention to interlibrary loan requests for microfilm copies of papers held by the Archives mitigated not being located near one of their regional centers. The handsome look of the publication reflects the vision and creativity of Don Ackland of Legacy Communications, Inc. and Roger L. Morrison, designer. Tom Burkett kept the text on track.

Many volunteers devoted numerous hours to advancing the research of Arms, the documentation of the Academy's collection, and the finalization of the collection checklist. Fran D'Ycaza and Emily Walker labored in the Academy's library while Elaine Chang provided important assistance in cataloguing the collection. Pearl Kadota, Teresa R. Knox, and Sun Namkung contributed their expertise essential to the preparation of the checklist's typescript and its proofreading. Linda Sjogren, Marcia Morse, and James F. Jensen also lent their skills to the cataloguing and catalogue project. This publication becomes a reality due to their willing participation.

The assistance of Academy staff also underlies the publication of this catalogue, including the efforts of W. Donald Brown, publications editor; Anne T. Seaman, librarian; Sanna Saks Deutsch, Academy registrar; David de la Torre, associate director; and Cathy A. Ng, assistant to the associate director. Special thanks are due Philip Roach, researcher of Asian art, for discussing with the author Japanese aesthetics as well as *ukiyo-e* and *shin hanga* prints, and Tibor Franyo, photographer, for undertaking the photography of the collection. George R. Ellis, director, is owed particular acknowledgment for his willingness to allow the author to set aside time unencumbered by other obligations to prepare the catalogue's manuscript. I thank them all most heartily. *J.S.*

John Taylor Arms and Plates of Perfect Beauty:
An Introduction

*For exactly twenty-one years I have visualized a plate of perfect
beauty and, in my own way and according to the dictates of my own
impulses, I have striven to achieve it. I gave up hope, a long while
ago, of ever etching a perfect plate, and concentrated upon attain-
ing one perfect passage. Now this seems vain, and perhaps it is no
exaggeration to say that, before I finally put aside needle and acid,
I pray that I may etch one perfect single line.*[1]

With these words written in 1937, John Taylor Arms (1887–1953)
described his pursuit of beauty through the etched medium. Over the
course of a career which spanned five decades, he put needle to plate
and published 429 prints, primarily etchings.[2]

Arms is considered one of the most eloquent exponents of the graphic arts in the
United States during the first half of the 20th century. Although he worked with diverse
subjects, he achieved greatest acclaim for architectural themes inspired by the medieval
monuments of Europe as well as the urban profile of New York City. An architect by
training, he felt a passionate affinity with the built environment of the Western world,
especially the richness and beauty of 12th- through 15th-century European Gothic
structures. An early gift of almost twenty prints from Eliza Lefferts and Charles
Montague Cooke, Jr., provided the foundation of the collection of work by Arms at the
Honolulu Academy of Arts. The subsequent donation of 170 prints by Helen T. and
Richard H. Hagemeyer have made it one of the finest public holdings in the nation and
a resource that allows the close examination of Arms' career.

Arms was born and raised in Washington, D.C. After graduation from
Lawrenceville School in New Jersey in 1905, he began studies at Princeton University
for a career in law and then transferred in 1907 to the School of Architecture at the
Massachusetts Institute of Technology. Earning his undergraduate degree in 1911 and
an M.S. degree in 1912, Arms was prepared by his studies in classical design and experience in draftsmanship for a career in architecture. Two years as an architectural
draftsperson in the New York firm of Jean Carrère and Thomas Hastings preceded
Arms' formation of an architectural partnership with Cameron Clark in 1914.[3]

Arms married Dorothy Noyes in 1913, and that year she gave him a twelve-dollar
etching kit as a Christmas present.[4] Arms took up etching as a hobby and mastered its
multiple steps as a self-taught artist. His first efforts were copies of prints by European
masters such as Johan Barthold Jongkind.[5] Creating seventeen plates before World War I,
Arms published his first print, *Sunlight and Shadow*, in 1915 (F.1, fig. 3).[6] Its representation

of a medieval house front with an overhanging gable introduced architecture as the theme that links most of the work in his *oeuvre*. In 1919, after serving in the Navy during World War I, Arms withdrew from his architectural partnership and took up print-making on a full-time basis.

Arms' early prints dating from before the war to about 1923 demonstrate his attempts to master various graphic media and means of representation and to address different subjects of interest. With etching as well as drypoint, aquatint, lithography, and even mezzotint, Arms rendered poetic views of sailboats on calm waters (pl. 8, figs. 19–20), idyllic views of rural Maine (figs. 11–13), and strikingly composed views of ships and airplanes engaged in wartime patrols (pl. 7, fig. 18). He also maintained his focus on architectural subjects, rendering picturesque views and street scenes of Europe's medieval towns (figs. 3, 4, 6, 8). Impressed with New York City, Arms was inspired to consider the beauty and engineering miracles represented by the Brooklyn Bridge, the grandeur of the city's skyline and skyscrapers, and the quick rhythms of city life as seen in the heart of the midtown bustle along Forty-Second Street (pls. 11–14, figs. 26–27). Many of these early images comprise the first series of prints with which Arms began to organize his *oeuvre*—the *Gable Series, Aquatint Series, Maine Series*, and *New York Series*.

Beginning in the 1920s, Arms traveled with his wife, and at times his whole family, through Europe on pilgrimages to Gothic architectural monuments. The soaring towers, radiant facades, imaginative sculpture, richly detailed ornamentation, and harmony of the whole came to symbolize for him humankind's finest technical achievements and highest spiritual aspirations. In his prints Arms sought to capture what he called the "Gothic Spirit" and to express the "enduring value of beauty" as seen in the glorious buildings of England, France, northern Italy, and Spain.[7] Many of his finest prints, remarkable for their compositional boldness, hyper-clarity, and technical virtuosity, are at the heart of the most important series of prints that preoccupied him for the remainder of his career—the *Gargoyle Series, Spanish Church Series, French Church Series, English Series*, and *Italian Series*. Paris and Venice among other sites provided Arms with subjects that inspired him to reach for plates of perfect beauty. They proffered the grand conception of cathedrals such as Notre Dame, with the timeless patience of its gargoyles, and the shimmering light and exquisite architectural ornamentation of Venetian canals.

Arms approached his work with a dazzling technical facility. Eschewing standard etching tools for the delicacy of sewing needles, he carefully drew and etched his images, at times clocking in as many as 2,000 hours on one work alone![8] A superb draftsperson and designer, Arms approached his views with a masterful sense of bold composition. He carefully delineated forms, brought out significant detail with painstaking linework, and infused his prints with an intangible spirituality. If linework and design provide the foundation of his prints, the luminous play of light and shadow across weathered stone, rippling water, and carved detail give them life and expression.

An individual of boundless energy and unswerving focus, Arms lived, breathed, and no doubt, dreamed prints. Over the course of some forty years, he also built a remark-able graphic arts collection that numbered nearly five thousand etchings, engravings, woodcuts, lithographs, and drawings by printmakers of the past five hundred years.[9] While making his living as a printmaker, Arms also committed himself to a second career as an advocate for the graphic arts. As a curator, author, speaker, correspondent, collector, volunteer consultant, board member, and leader, Arms played an important role in the promotion of American graphic arts of this century and stood as an early spokesman for artistic freedom of expression. If seeing is believing, Arms was also responsible for the conversion of hundreds of individuals to the wonder of printmaking.

He maintained a busy schedule demonstrating the etching process to school, library, museum, art, community, and business audiences. The prints created during his more than 150 demonstrations make up yet another series of prints, the *Demonstration Series.*

Praised as an American medievalist by his admirers, considered old-fashioned by his detractors because he refused to abandon the precise representation of the physical world and adopt a more personal means of expression, Arms combined sensitivity, eloquence, and technical excellence in his art.[10] Deeply committed to his subjects and medium, he strove to create a plate of perfect beauty through which he might celebrate the human spirit. The chapters that follow address Arms' life and *oeuvre* and suggest how close he came to his goal.[11]

1. John Taylor Arms, "Self Estimate," in *Twenty-One Years of Drawing, A Retrospective Exhibition of the Work of John Taylor Arms, N.A., A.R.E., P.S.A.E.,* exh. cat. (New York: The Grand Central Art Galleries, 1937), p. 11.

2. One published and two unpublished typescript catalogue raisonnés provide the most thorough documentation of Arms' graphic output: William Dolan Fletcher, *John Taylor Arms, A Man for All Time, The Artist and His Work* (The Sign of the Arrow, 1982); Ulrich Kropfl, "A Catalogue of the Work of John Taylor Arms, N.A., A.R.E., P.S.A.E.," 1971 (unpublished typescript in the Prints and Photographs Division of the Library of Congress, Washington, D.C.); John Taylor Arms and Dorothy Noyes Arms, "Descriptive Catalogue of the Work of John Taylor Arms," 2 vols., 1962 (unpublished typescript catalogue in the Prints Division of the New York Public Library, prepared from records compiled by the artist, edited by his wife, and completed after her death by his former secretaries, May Bradshaw Hays and Marie Probstfield, under the sponsorship of the New York Public Library). Variations in the documentation of Arms' *oeuvre* appear in the three catalogues; this author refers to Fletcher's work as the standard record.

3. Arms worked on Carrère and Hastings' plans for the Henry Clay Frick House (now the Frick Collection) and the Pulitzer Fountain (also known as the Plaza Fountain), both on Fifth Avenue in New York City. See Carl Zigrosser, "John Taylor Arms," in *The Artist in America, Twenty-Four Close-Ups of Contemporary Printmakers* (New York: Alfred A. Knopf, 1942), pp. 24–25.

4. Dorothy Noyes Arms was Arms' constant companion throughout his life and collaborated with him on different publication projects. As author of several essays about Arms, she also served as one of his most important promoters. See Dorothy Noyes Arms and John Taylor Arms, *Churches of France* (New York: The Macmillan Company, 1929); Dorothy Noyes Arms and John Taylor Arms, *Hill Towns and Cities of Northern Italy* (New York: The Macmillan Company, 1932); and Dorothy Noyes Arms, "John Taylor Arms, Modern Mediævalist," *The Print Collector's Quarterly* 21, no. 2 (April 1934), pp. 126–141.

5. Arms, "Self Estimate," pp. 7–8.

6. "F" numbers cited after the first reference to each Arms print refer to the catalogue raisonné number assigned by Fletcher.

7. Zigrosser, "The Artist in America," p. 27; letter from John Taylor Arms to Carl Zigrosser, dated Fairfield, CT, Sept. 3, 1941 (Carl Zigrosser Papers, 4613:734, Archives of American Art, Smithsonian Institution, Washington, D.C.; henceforth "AAA").

8. Ben L. Bassham, *John Taylor Arms, American Etcher,* exh. cat. (Madison, WI: Elvehjem Art Center, University of Wisconsin-Madison, 1975), p. 29. According to Arms' records, he spent 2,172 hours creating *"Spanish Profile," Palencia,* 1950 (F.418).

9. Bassham, *John Taylor Arms,* p. 35, FN 11. After Arms' death, his Connecticut neighbors, Ward M. and Mariam C. Canaday, purchased the collection and presented it to the College of Wooster, Ohio, in 1967. See Robert H. Getscher, *Félix Bracquemond and the Etching Process,* exh. cat. (Wooster, Ohio: The College of Wooster, 1974), p. 5.

10. See S. William Pelletier, "John Taylor Arms: An American Mediaevalist," *The Georgia Review* 30, no. 4 (Winter, 1976), pp. 908–987 and "New Exhibitions of the Week, J.T. Arms: Twenty-One Years of Drawing," *Art News* 35, no. 16 (Jan. 16, 1937), p. 16.

11. The chapters that follow do not pretend to be a comprehensive survey of Arms' work and career. Published in association with a collection catalogue, they delve into issues reflected by the prints in the Honolulu Academy of Arts' holdings. However, the collection is extensive, with fine impressions for the most part of Arms' graphic *oeuvre.* It provides strong representation of most of Arms' print series and other printmaking efforts. Since the Academy's collection does not include an impression from the *U.S. Navy Series,* that group of work is not mentioned in the text.

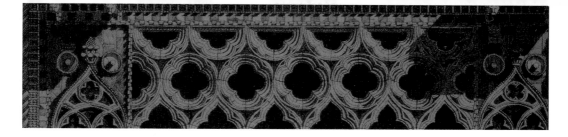

The Early Prints, 1915–1922

When Arms took up etching in 1914, the course of American art, including printmaking, was in transition. At the turn of the century, artists were grappling with history, past traditions, and paths to the future. The year 1913 marked the first presentation of European modernism in New York City, when works by the French Post-Impressionists, Symbolists, Fauvists, and other progressive artists appeared in the Armory Show. Traditional representational perspectives were beginning to give way to different means of expression. Robert Henri, John Sloan, and other members of the Ashcan School took urban life as their topic; Arthur B. Davies, Alfred Stieglitz, and his circle of friends assumed more personal, non-objective approaches in their art. French Impressionism remained an influence with painters such as Childe Hassam, while cubism provided an exciting new way to look at the world for Max Weber. Japanese art, especially wood-block prints, led many American artists such as Arthur Wesley Dow to adopt new aesthetic principles.

Related changes also marked the development of printmaking, with Americans following a European lead. During the middle decades of the nineteeth century, France experienced a printmaking revival. Théodore Rousseau, Charles-François Daubigny, Adolphe Appian (fig. 1), Charles-Émile Jacque, and others associated with the Barbizon School were the first French artists to revitalize the art of etching after a late eighteenth-century hiatus. As in their paintings, they rendered picturesque landscapes and rural scenes infused with a poetic sense of life lived in harmony with nature. Charles Meryon, Maxime Lalanne, and other French artists discovered in etching a means to create evocative views of Paris and urban life.

Figure 1
Adolphe Appian,
1819–1898, France
*New Pond Near Creys
(Isère)*, 1864
Etching
5⁷⁄₁₆ x 10½ in.
(13.8 x 26.7 cm)
Honolulu Academy
of Arts
Gift of Anna Rice
Cooke, 1927 (5192)

The etching revival took hold in England during the third quarter of the nineteenth century, with the American expatriate James McNeill Whistler and his English brother-in-law Francis Seymour Haden adopting the medium. Whistler recognized in etching a means of exploring his personal aesthetic, and Haden captured with his picturesque landscapes the changing moods of the British countryside. Whistler's prints were known in the United States by 1862, and Haden arrived for a lecture tour of the country in 1882.[1] Both printmakers were highly influential in England and the United States. Haden was a particularly energetic and articulate driving force on both sides of the Atlantic in promoting the recognition of printmaking as a legitimate means of original, creative expression.

For most of the nineteenth century, American printmaking took the form of commercial lithography and reproductive wood engraving. In the last quarter of the century, American collectors and artists became aware of the etching revival in Europe and developed an appreciation themselves. They generated an active graphic arts community, supported by etching clubs and societies, exhibitions, lectures, new commercial galleries, growing public and private collections, and new periodicals.[2] Landscapists such as Thomas Moran, James D. Smillie, and Stephen Parrish together with artists interested in urban, especially European, subjects, including Joseph Pennell, Charles Mielatz, and Otto Bacher, led the American etching revival with their representational imagery. An internationally prominent and prolific printmaker producing over 1,500 etchings and lithographs, Pennell is undoubtedly the best-known of American printmakers rendering American and European city views. Pennell traveled through Europe and the United States, rendering images of cities old and new. Early in his career he published pictorial Old World scenes from the Alhambra to Zaandam as parts of numerous print series (*Spanish* and *Holland* series in this case). Etching, enjoyed because of the facile, personal draftsmanship and spontaneous effects it allows, was the preferred graphic technique at the time. By the end of the century, however, as leaders of the revival died or their interests and that of the art community changed, etching lost its support and all but disappeared from the American art scene.[3]

Although John Marin created etchings as early as 1905, the years 1915 and 1916 marked a renewal of American printmaking, as many artists created their first etchings or lithographs. Martin Lewis and Edward Hopper first put needle to plate in 1915, as did Stuart Davis and Jan Matulka the following year.[4] The publication of the first issue of *The Print-Collector's Quarterly* in 1911, the renewed growth of museum and private print collections, and significant representation of prints in the Armory Show in 1913 and then again at the Panama-Pacific International Exposition in San Francisco

Figure 2
Donald Shaw
MacLaughlan,
1876–1938,
United States
Ruelle Pigeonnière,
1903
Etching
4³/₁₆ x 2⁵/₈ in.
(10.6 x 6.7 cm)
Honolulu Academy
of Arts
Gift of Eliza Lefferts
and Charles
Montague Cooke,
Jr., 1927 (7007)

in 1915 all reflected growing support for the graphic arts. Printmaking organizations again became active with the founding of the Association of American Etchers in 1913 and the first exhibition of the Brooklyn Society of Etchers in 1916. The first part of the twentieth century enjoyed new diversity in choice of subject matter, conceptual framework, styles, and printmaking media.[5] While John Marin, Martin Lewis, and Edward Hopper responded to urban life and the built environment by developing personal and progressive styles, a second generation of American etchers extended the pictorial tradition of Pennell, Bacher, Mielatz, and other late-nineteenth-century print-makers. Ernest D. Roth, Lester Hornby, and Donald Shaw MacLaughlan followed in their footsteps, etching picturesque views of European cities and towns such as MacLaughlan's *Ruelle Pigeonnière* (fig. 2).[6] Such charming views of Old World towns and landscapes appealed to traditionalist collectors such as Eliza Lefferts and Charles Montague Cooke, first donors of prints by Pennell, Roth, Mielatz, and MacLaughlan as well as Arms to the Honolulu Academy of Arts. Arms published *Sunlight and Shadow* (fig. 3) as his first print in 1915, having probably based his view of aging half-timbered and gabled house fronts on France's medieval Lisieux.[7] With this print Arms extended the American architectural pictorial tradition and became part of the artistic ferment characterizing newly developing American printmaking.

Although documentation of Arms' early years as a printmaker is scarce, the examination of his early work, prints created up to around 1923, suggests that as a self-taught artist he looked for inspiration and guidance in a number of directions. Arms experimented with different printmaking media and types of subjects and responded to the work of many masters as he established the course of his mature development. While at this time he created the majority of his plates with etching, he also worked with aquatint, drypoint, mezzotint, and lithography. Just as his reputation as an etcher of meticulous architectural subjects is well founded, Arms only developed this focus after creating significant bodies of work devoted to subjects as diverse as rural Maine land-scapes, sailboats on still bodies of water, and airplanes in flight. A consideration of his early prints will make clear that Arms, despite the lack of formal training, did not work in a vacuum as an outsider. An educated man and avid collector of prints, he found inspiration in the art of Rembrandt, the Barbizon School, Whistler, Haden, Charles Meryon, perhaps even Arthur Wesley Dow.

It was only natural that Arms, trained as an architect with professional experience in drafting and traditional Western architectural styles, established an early interest in architectural subjects. In an autobiographical statement published in 1930, Arms related:

> *In my early days as an etcher, as I took stock of the mediæval towns of France and Italy and Spain, the subjects which attracted my attention were for the most part of an intimate nature, an old gable here, a door-way there, or a bit of rambling street with its quaint shop fronts and inevitable carts. These furnished the material for many a sketch and were, so to speak, the first chapters of my etched history.[8]*

Sunlight and Shadow was the first of many small etchings depicting intimate views of crumbling medieval gables and housefronts, irregular rooflines and overhanging storeys, picturesque street corners, and narrow streets derived from Arms' earliest visits to Rouen, Lisieux, and other French cities with medieval roots.[9] A comparison of *Sunlight and Shadow* with *Lisieux: Gable in the Grande Rue*, 1916 (F.3, fig. 4) and *A Roof in Thiers*, 1921 (F.115, pl. 1) illustrates his growing mastery of the etching process

Figure 3
Sunlight and Shadow,
1915
Etching
5¹⁵/₁₆ x 4 in.
(15.1 x 10.2 cm)
Gift of Richard H.
and Helen T.
Hagemeyer, 1989
(20,606)

and developing artistic vision. Over the course of creating these three plates, Arms achieved greater sophistication in his contrasts of light and shade, especially evident in the shadows of the overhangs in the last two prints. He also fixed his subjects more firmly within the rectangular framework of his plate. In *Sunlight and Shadow* and more particularly *Gable in the Grande Rue*, the house fronts float in the center of the plate partially enframed by sweeping, curving strokes of the needle, distanced temporally and spatially from the viewer. Arms elaborated the roof and house front more fully in *A Roof in Thiers* with greater detail and extended the image out to the edges of the plate. Such attention to detail and more thorough working of the plate's entire surface hint at the same qualities that appear in his mature work. Arms assigned each of these prints to his *Gable Series*, one of the nineteen series into which he divided his work during the length of his career. The organization of his prints into formal series, his building of a *Gable Series, Italian Series, French Church Series*, etc., deepens his connection with turn-of-the-century traditions. To be successful at this time, printmakers were expected to have etched, at least once, a series of European views.[10]

As Arms continued to work with architectural subjects, his interests extended beyond the work of Roth, MacLaughlan, and other second-generation masters of the etching revival. That he acquired in 1913 the first print of a collection which eventually was to number nearly five thousand works—he purchased an etching of Benares, India, by Ernest S. Lumsden[11]—indeed suggests an early fascination with the work of various printmakers. Later writings by Arms confirm a deep appreciation for the power and beauty of prints by the French master Charles Meryon and the American expatriate James McNeill Whistler, an appreciation which is also evidenced in his early prints. Arms once referred to Meryon as "the supreme interpreter of architecture through the medium of the bitten line," and Whistler as "one of the greatest masters of etching the world has produced."[12] In the prints of Meryon, Arms found inspiration for what he called the "expression of the spirit of the subject, and not its mere physical appearance."[13] The prints of Whistler opened his eyes to some of the formal qualities that would preoccupy him throughout his career, as they "are unsurpassed for the harmony of their design, the exquisiteness and sensitiveness of their drawing, and the subtlety of their printing."[14]

Meryon, one of the most important figures and remarkable personalities in the history of French printmaking, turned to art after an early career in the French Navy. He is best known for *Etchings of Paris*, a set of prints begun in 1850, which depicts Parisian landmarks, street scenes, and views along the River Seine. Meryon focused on the city's medieval monuments, such as Notre Dame and the Palais de Justice, and architectural details, including the house and turret rendered in *Tourelle, Rue de la Tixéranderie*, 1852 (fig. 5). Meryon's interest in medieval structures, street scenes, and architectural details (facades, roof lines, gables, and dormer windows) must have attracted Arms. Important elements in Meryon's *oeuvre* included: careful linework, fully worked plates, a striking sense of contrast, an almost animate quality to the shadowed windows and doorways, a rather haunting mysteriousness, and small figures vitalizing the compositions. Many of these same qualities make a tentative appearance in Arms' early depiction of European architectural subjects

such as *A Roof in Thiers*, continue through the 20s in prints such as *Lescure, Une Tour des Remparts*, 1928 (F.217, fig. 6), and reach complete expression in mature works such as *Venetian Filigree*, 1931 (F.235, fig. 44).

Arms commented that for him the plates in Meryon's *Etchings of Paris* "are among the greatest of man's achievements on the copper—powerful, restrained, concentrated, beautiful in their clarity, rich in their inner meaning, faultless in their execution."[15] Most important of all for Arms is what he recognized as the set's spiritual power. Arms believed that a work's essential spirit, rather than its outward aspect, was paramount. He commented that the "twelve masterpieces" in the series make it "a monument unique in its sensitive, imaginative, and deeply spiritual expression of architectural form and meaning."[16]

If Arms turned to Meryon for spiritual guidance, he recognized Whistler for his technical brilliance and compositional innovations. Arms admired Whistler's two early suites of prints, the *French Set* (also known as *Twelve Etchings from Nature*) published in 1858 and the *Thames Set* of 1871. The former group is comprised of portraits of Seymour Haden's children, images of Parisian slums, and scenes of rural poverty in the

Figure 6
Lescure, Une Tour des Remparts, 1928
Etching
6⁷/₁₆ x 3¹⁵/₁₆ in.
(16.4 x 10.0 cm)
Gift of Richard H. and Helen T. Hagemeyer, 1990
(20,848)

Rhine Valley. The latter consists of Whistler's "realist" views of London's Thames River and the life and labor along its banks. Of the etchings, Arms wrote his appreciation, "Both series are characterized by loving attention to detail and textural quality, beautiful lighting, an unerring feeling for composition, fluent and expressive drawing, and a remarkable blending of strength and delicacy."[17]

The lightly etched lines and "unfinished" sketchiness of Arms' *Sunlight and Shadow* (fig. 3) and *Lisieux: Gable in the Grande Rue* (fig. 4) recall Whistler's style.[18] The compositional format of many of Arms' prints, both early and mature, derive from design concepts discovered in the suites of Whistler's prints. Take, for example, Whistler's *Street at Saverne*, 1858 (fig. 7), a nocturnal view of an all-but-deserted

Figure 7
James McNeill Whistler, 1834–1903, United States
Street at Saverne, 1858
Etching
8¹/₈ x 6¹/₈ in.
(20.6 x 15.6 cm)
The Minneapolis Institute of Arts

narrow street lined with aging medieval houses, almost animate yet blank-faced with their shadowed and empty windows and doorways. The print, as striking with its dramatic contrast of light and shade as it is with its boldly oblique and accelerated perspective, was an unusual one for the time. Arms etched in 1919 a similar street scene characterized by similar qualities: *Dol—Old Houses in La Grande Rue*, 1919 (F.30, fig. 8). Oblique perspectives and exaggerated recession recur throughout Arms' architectural imagery, as in *West Forty-Second Street* of the following year (F.41, fig. 26), *La Tour d'Horloge, Dinan* of 1932 (F.246, pl. 2), even *In Memoriam* of 1939 (F.317, pl. 16), one of his finest prints.

Equally pervasive in Arms' printmaking is his interest in a tunnel-like, frame-within-a-frame format, as strikingly worked out by Whistler in the *French Set* and *Thames Set*.[19] In a radically constructed picture space, Whistler maintained the oblique and accelerated perspective described above, framed his scenes with architectural truncations, and structured the vistas through progressively receding light and dark zones, archways, and doorways.[20] Whistler's *The Lime-Burner*, 1859 (fig. 9), one of the sixteen prints in the *Thames Set* and identified by Arms as one of the outstanding works in the suite,[21] presents a forceful interpretation of the format. The work is extraordinary for its geometric abstraction, spatial flow, tonal contrast, juxtaposition of near and far, and counterpoint of opposing forms.

Figure 8
Dol—Old Houses in La Grande Rue,
1919
Etching
$7^{7}/_{16}$ x $9^{11}/_{16}$ in.
(18.9 x 24.6 cm)
Gift of Richard H. and Helen T. Hagemeyer, 1991
(21,154)

Arms grappled with the complexities of this compositional format as early as 1919 in *A Winding Street, Mans* (F.31) and *An Old Courtyard, Italy*, 1920 (F.54, fig. 10). In the latter work, he suggested spatial depth with the oblique recession of opposing stone walls, seemingly quickened by the upward diagonal of the staircases. An archway in the middle distance enframes two figures silhouetted against additional buildings beyond. In this work Arms effectively joined the scene's underlying geometry, its architectural truncations, contrast of sunlit and shadowed spaces, and repetition and counterpointing of doorways, windows, and staircases. *An Old Courtyard* is one of his most compositionally sophisticated early works. The format appears in subsequent prints, especially images in the *Demonstration Series*,[22] with variations in plates such as *Abside de la Cathédrale de Saint Pierre et Saint Paul, Troyes*, 1929 (F.224, pl. 3). In addition to its technical brilliance, this work is particularly notable for the bold division of foreground and background into shadowed and sunlit areas, its striking juxtaposition of open and blind gateway and gallery arches, and effective geometric architectural abstraction.

Arms' appreciation for the graphic work of Meryon and Whistler may also have led to an aesthetic interest of a more technical nature—a fascination with paper. The etching revival introduced many artists to the rich variation of tone, texture, weight, and weave that characterized different papers of Western and Japanese manufacture. Indeed, the enjoyment Arms' predecessors found in diverse paper types is well documented. Meryon began to hunt for antique European papers and lustrous Japanese stock in the early 1850s. Whistler followed suit, searching for loose leaves of paper and old books with blank sheets that he could remove and use in his printing.[23] Arms also collected and used old paper in addition to the diverse modern papers he acquired. A baptismal register of 1708 from Middletown, Pennsylvania, provided Arms with the earliest paper on which he is known to have printed.[24] A close examination of his works sometimes reveals gilded edges or acid stains on three edges and a fourth irregular margin as characterize a page removed from an old book. Other sheets bear inked inscriptions, again indicating an older source.[25] Arms even learned to make his own paper.[26]

In an article Arms prepared about the printing process, he articulated his admiration for old paper, commenting that it "is very beautiful to print on, not because it is of a better quality...but because the 'size' has worn off...and the paper has assumed, in time, a tone which cannot be obtained by staining modern paper."[27] Arms' *oeuvre*

Figure 9
James McNeill Whistler, 1834–1903, United States
The Lime-Burner, 1859
Etching, drypoint
10 x 7 in.
(25.4 x 17.8 cm)
Honolulu Academy of Arts
Gift of Anna Rice Cooke, 1927 (5802)

Figure 10
An Old Courtyard,
Italy, 1920
Etching, aquatint
$7^7/_{16}$ x $6^3/_4$ in.
(18.9 x 17.1 cm)
Gift of Richard H.
and Helen T.
Hagemeyer, 1989
(20,615)

Figure 11
The Trapper's Home,
1920
Etching
5$\frac{11}{16}$ x 8$\frac{13}{16}$ in.
(14.4 x 22.4 cm)
Gift of Richard H.
and Helen T.
Hagemeyer, 1988
(20,483)

Figure 12
"Pete" and "Topsy,"
1920
Etching
5$\frac{9}{16}$ x 6$\frac{3}{8}$ in.
(14.1 x 16.2 cm)
Gift of Richard H.
and Helen T.
Hagemeyer, 1989
(20,625)

John Taylor Arms

includes prints on aged and contemporary American, European, and Japanese papers ranging in weight from the thinnest of tissue to the stiffness of card stock. Although the majority of his work is printed on standard neutral tones—white, ivory, cream, etc.— his prints also appear on yellow, green, blue, and gray colored stock. The Academy's collection of Arms prints hints at the wide range of weights, textures, and tones that mark the papers found in his graphic *oeuvre*. For instance, Arms used a sheet of antique paper with a delicate green-gray cast for the Academy's impression of *Abside de la Cathédrale de Saint Pierre et Saint Paul, Troyes*, a warmly toned Japanese tissue in *Rodez*, 1927 (F.189, pl. 15), a sheet of modern green paper for *Stockholm*, 1940 (F.346, pl. 4), a modern sheet of darker green for *Crystal and Jade*, 1936–40 (F.301, pl. 5), and a subtle blue-green sheet for *Stokesay Castle*, 1942 (F.369, pl. 19).

Aware of the breadth of effects possible with different papers, Arms experimented throughout his career with multiple sheet types within a given edition. For instance, the Academy's two sequential impressions of *The Trapper's Home*, 1920 (F.60, fig. 11), appear on sheets of laid paper comparable in their weight and texture but different in tone. The off-white color of one sheet creates a cooler, more brilliant effect than the warmth of the cream-colored sheet.[28]

During the first years of their marriage, Arms and his wife spent summers in Maine before establishing a summer studio in North Pomfret, Vermont. Their time in these northern back woods provided sketches and ideas for another group of prints, the *Maine Series*. This body of work includes approximately 30 etchings; all but one dates from 1920. The prints illustrated here, *The Trapper's Home, "Pete" and "Topsy,"* 1920 (F.72, fig. 12), and *Beaver House*, 1920 (F.88, fig. 13), bear witness to many of the themes that recur in the *Maine Series*—intimate views of woodland corners, quiet ponds, weathered cabins, an occasional outdoorsman. Arms' treatment of the scenes is

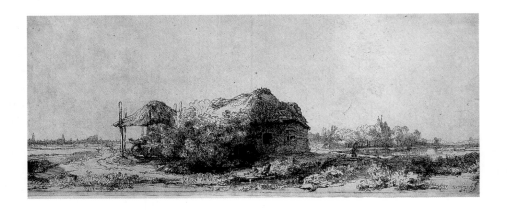

Figure 14
Rembrandt
Harmensz van Rijn,
1606–1669,
Holland
*Landscape with a
Cottage and Hay-
Barn,* 1641
Etching
5⅛ x 12¾ in.
(13.0 x 32.4 cm)
The Metropolitan
Museum of Art
Gift of George Coe
Graves, The Sylmaris
Collection, 1920
(20,465)

unselfconscious; their fresh and agile drawing style, pleasing sense of contrast, and stable compositions match the unprepossessing and picturesque nature of the landscapes.

Examining different traditions of printmaking at this early point in his career, Arms may have reached back in time to the work of Rembrandt, the seventeenth-century Dutch artist Arms referred to as the "supreme master of the etcher's art."[29] Arms recognized Rembrandt's landscape subjects as among the artist's most beautiful prints and noted in particular *Landscape with a Cottage and Hay-Barn* (fig. 14).[30] Rembrandt presented this subject, three figures outside an aging Dutch cottage nestled within the embrace of a few trees, with spontaneous linework, a gentle mood, and a sympathetic appreciation of country life. With his rural subjects, scribbly style, and quiet atmosphere, Rembrandt either inspired Arms directly or indirectly through his nineteenth-century followers, the members of the Barbizon School and England's Seymour Haden.

Just as Arms found inspiration for his views of medieval European towns in the work of the nineteenth-century etching revival, so too did he for his depictions of the Maine wilderness. Interested as he was in printmaking, Arms must have been aware of the picturesque rural scenes created by early nineteenth-century members of the Barbizon School or comparable subjects rendered by Seymour Haden, who worked throughout the second half of the century. Barbizon School artists such as Charles-

Figure 15
Francis Seymour
Haden, 1818–1910,
England
*Shere Mill Pond, No.
II (Large Plate),*
1860 and later
Etching, drypoint
7¹⁄₁₆ x 13⅛ in.
(17.9 x 33.3 cm)
Honolulu Academy
of Arts
Gift of Edith G.
Manuel, 1943
(12,020)

Émile Jacque and Charles-François Daubigny as well as Haden were less interested in the accurate, detailed representation of a specific subject than in the discovery of nature's picturesque qualities and the evocation of mood. Haden's representation of *Shere Mill Pond,* 1860 (fig. 15), described by Arms as one of his most splendid achievements,[31] typifies the naturalness of scene and easy fluidity of linework for which Haden is celebrated today. Prints such as this would have inspired Arms as he worked with his Maine subjects which, as does *Shere Mill,* carry within their quiet picturesqueness a nostalgic appreciation for the type of countryside falling victim to the new century's urban and industrial needs. Arms' *Maine Series* extends a late nineteenth-century appreciation of the simple, honest values of a rural, pre-modern existence.

In addition to turning to the tradition of Western printmaking for inspiration during the early years of his career, Arms also experimented with other graphic techniques, seeming to search for the process best suited to his own vision. He published two drypoints and one mezzotint at this time and created (although did not publish) eight lithographs. Arms' investigations into aquatint were of more sustained interest as he etched around forty plates with this tonal process.

Among Arms' first thirty-eight published prints, his two drypoints are views of New York City's skyline, the first from the Brooklyn Bridge and the second from the Staten Island Ferry. In *New York from Staten Island Ferry,* 1917 (F.14, fig. 16), a small image measuring only 1½ x 3¹⁵/₁₆ inches, the irregular profile and reflection of the buildings and ships appear sketchily rendered in the center of the plate. In addition to commenting that "this plate is the first of the only two plates I ever executed in pure drypoint," Arms also commented that "drypoint has been used very sparingly, as reinforcement, in a very few other of my plates."[32] Unfortunately, Arms did not elaborate on why he did not continue to work in the medium.

Three years later, Arms created his first and only pure mezzotint, *Moonlight, Rangeley Lake,* 1920 (F.65, pl. 6). The Maine subject, shoreline composition, and 1920 date relate it to the other works in Arms' *Maine Series.* In burnishing this image into the pitted plate, Arms captured the soft tonal transitions and enveloping shadows of a moonlit evening. Dorothy Noyes Arms commented very briefly on Arms' mezzotint effort. She wrote that *Moonlight, Rangeley Lake* "was merely an experiment—and the artist did not enjoy working in this medium."[33] Alas, once again, information documenting Arms' dissatisfaction with the process does not exist.

In 1921 Arms tried his hand at lithography, creating eight images that relate in subject to his other early prints. In addition to rendering log cabins in Maine and the New York City skyline, he also selected European subjects such as the unidentified hill

Figure 17
Castles in the Air,
1921
Lithograph
15½ x 10⅜ in.
(39.4 x 26.4 cm)
Gift of Richard H.
and Helen T.
Hagemeyer, 1991
(21,205)

John Taylor Arms

town depicted in *Castles in the Air*, 1921 (F.436, fig. 17). Arms trained under the well-known lithographer Bolton Brown in order to learn the planographic process. It appears that Arms was not pleased with the lithographs he created, calling them "strictly student work" which "has been seen by a few people."[34]

Arms first introduced aquatint into his prints in a rather tentatively composed and etched French street scene of 1916, *Rue des Matelots, Rouen* (F.12). Three years later, when relying on aquatint for the rendering of a variety of different subjects, Arms initiated his *Aquatint Series* with two cohesive bodies of aquatint prints—dramatic scenes of ships and airplanes during wartime and exquisitely elegant views of sailboats on calm waters. Arms concluded these groups in 1920 and sporadically continued to use the process up to 1947.

Prints such as *"S.C.'s" on Night Patrol*, 1920 (F.43, pl. 7) and *Wasps*, 1920 (F.51, fig. 18) derive from Arms' navy service during World War I. The former print depicts two submarine chasers meeting at night and exchanging signals. The vessel on the left is caught in the searchlight of the craft on the far right, with its signalman and gunner revealed in bold silhouette. *Wasps* presents two fighter aircraft on patrol with searchlight beams behind them. Arms wrote that such images "served as records of my vivid experi-

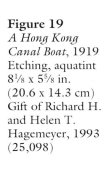

ences when my mind was full of navigation and of the hunt, through endless days and nights, for submarines."[35] With control of the finely granulated tonal effects of aquatint, Arms built bold almost abstract designs predicated on the contrast of flat planes of tone and strong, simplified shapes. The luminous midnight-blue ink with which Arms printed the plates contributes to the eerie drama of the scenes.

A consideration of the Academy's holdings of aquatint prints of sailboats reveals Arms' rapid mastery of this tonal process. *A Hong Kong Canal Boat*, 1919 (F.23, fig. 19) and *The Harbor at Aden*, 1919 (F.24), among the earliest prints in the group, join etching and aquatint, but the blending of the two is not as sure, not as completely finessed as in later prints. The linework is more obvious and the handling of the aquatint is more simplistic.

Figure 20
The Butterfly, 1920
Etching, aquatint
10¼ x 7⅜ in.
(26.0 x 18.7 cm)
Gift of Richard H.
and Helen T.
Hagemeyer, 1993
(24,031)

Moonlight, Number One, 1920 (F.47, pl. 8) and *The Butterfly*, 1920 (F.48, fig. 20) represent Arms' total mastery of the medium. In both prints solitary sailboats appear becalmed, their reflections barely broken by the ripples of still water, their sails silhouetted against the distant horizon and mountains. Arms minimized linework and suggested detail, distance, and atmosphere through exquisitely graduated planes of tone. The aquatinting in *The Butterfly*, the delicacy with which the snow-covered peaks and the complexity of the shimmering waters are described, is a tour de force. The subtle tonal range of *Moonlight, Number One* underlies the refined beauty of the work.

Arms' aquatint etchings bear striking similarities to Japanese eighteenth- and nineteenth-century *ukiyo-e* and the first twentieth-century *shin hanga* woodblock prints (fig. 21).[36] As in Japanese prints, the beauty of Arms' aquatints, such as *Wasps* and *Moonlight, Number One*, resides in the subtly graduated flat areas of tone, soft hues, silhouetted and simplified shapes, tilted perspective, asymmetry, truncated forms, and the exaggerated juxtaposition of foreground and background. Even the strongly vertical shape of *Moonlight, Number One* speaks of the Japanese woodblock print tradition. One author

writing in 1920 about Arms' aquatints mentioned their Japonesque quality but went on to say that "Mr. Arms is not and never has been a student of Oriental art or to any marked degree influenced by it. They are a purely personal expression of his own ideas of design."[37] This denial of Arms' interest or awareness of Japanese printmaking has not been questioned since this article, and perhaps it is appropriate to do so.

With the opening of Japan in 1854, *ukiyo-e* prints flooded the Western world, and Japanese art appeared in American world's fairs, auctions, galleries, exhibitions, books, and interior design. By the 1880s Japanese art could be purchased in London and Paris as well as Boston, New York, Chicago, San Francisco, and elsewhere.[38] Hiroshige's *One Hundred Views of Edo*, 1856–7, one of the most popular *ukiyo-e* print series in the Western world, was printed in several editions and exported.[39] Americans and Europeans alike were fascinated with the "exotic" culture and way of seeing discovered in the woodblock images. Whistler's dependence on Japanese subjects and stylistic qualities is well documented, as is the comparable interest of many late-nineteenth-century French and American artists. Public and private collections of Japanese prints developed in many American cities. The New York Public Library received a gift of 1,763 *ukiyo-e* prints in 1901.[40] Beginning in 1900, Yoshida Hiroshi, one of Japan's best-known *shin hanga* printmakers, made with several colleagues the first of several trips to the United States for commercial exhibitions in Boston, New York, Detroit, Indianapolis, Saint Louis, and elsewhere.[41] Depictions of Japanese junks, reminiscent of the sailboats found in the prints of John Taylor Arms, was a recurrent subject in the work they exhibited (fig. 21).[42] Junks found their way into the printmaking of American artists such as Bertha Lum, who completed *Junks in Inland Sea* in 1908 (fig. 22). With the woodblock process,

Figure 23
Charles F. W.
Mielatz, 1864–1919,
b. Germany, act.
United States
Rainy Night,
Madison Square,
1890
Etching, aquatint
12⅝ x 9 in.
(32.1 x 22.9 cm)
Honolulu Academy
of Arts
Gift of Eliza Lefferts
and Charles
Montague Cooke,
Jr., 1927 (7020)

Japanese subject, and stylistic approach of her print, Lum drew directly on the Japanese printmaking tradition. Given the enthusiasm with which Japanese art was greeted in the United States and the seriousness with which Arms entered the printmaking community, he must have been familiar with Japanese printmaking. Why else would he have addressed an Asian subject as found in *A Hong Kong Canal Boat*? Why else would he title an aquatint image of a small fishing ship, silhouetted against what appears to be the New York City skyline in a composition related to his sailboat prints, *Drifting, Somewhere in the Orient*, 1919 (F.27)?

Even if Arms did not enjoy a direct acquaintance with Japanese art, he would not have had to look beyond turn-of-the-century artmaking in the United States to be exposed to its principles. Charles Mielatz, Joseph Pennell, and Martin Lewis among others evidenced an appreciation of Japanese prints in their intaglio and lithographic work (fig. 23); American woodblock printing spread through other artists such as Arthur Wesley Dow, B.J.O. Nordfeldt, and Edna Boies Hopkins. Even photography was not unaffected, as evocative prints by Alvin Langdon Coburn reveal. The Japonesque was an important ingredient in the American art scene at the end of the nineteenth and beginning of the twentieth centuries.

Similarities between Arms' aquatints and diagrams in Arthur Wesley Dow's revolutionary art-instruction text, *Composition*, invite speculation that Arms was familiar with its presentation of Japanese art principles. A painter, printmaker, and art educator, Dow applied Japanese theory to his own woodblock prints as early as 1895. Teaching at the Pratt Institute in Brooklyn, as well as New York's Arts Students League, and Teachers College at Columbia University, Dow spread ideas shaped by an appreciation for Japanese graphic design and *notan* (tonal or value relationships within a composition). Dow's influence spread further with the publication of *Composition* in 1899. This book ran through several editions and was the standard book used by art students, teachers, and amateurs such as Arms during the first decades of this century. The slim volume includes text on what Dow perceived to be the seminal elements of design, or what he called the "three structural elements with which harmonies may be built up,"—line, notan, and color.[43] In the book Dow took his reader through these elements and how they fit within principles of composition. Diagrams fill the volume, illustrating his concepts and the exercises he suggested his readers undertake. Diagrams of fruit and flowers growing on branches, trees juxtaposed against distant horizons, sailboats reflected in calm water, among other designs, are unmistakably based on Japanese printmaking (fig. 24). Their truncations of form, tilted perspectives, bold contrasts of foreground and background, even the elongated rectangular formats bespeak Dow's affinity for Japonism. A comparison of Arms' aquatints, such as *Moonlight, Number One* (pl. 8) and several of Dow's diagrams, such as the variations of sailboats on water, strongly suggest that Arms, learning about art, curious about different graphic techniques and different modes of vision, considered Dow and his teachings.

Several of Arms' early aquatints count among his finest prints. However, after immersing himself in the aquatint process in 1919 and 1920 and completing 27 such toned prints, Arms rarely returned to it. He planned to do a series of color aquatints that would illustrate "the history and development of the ship from the earliest times to the present day,"[44] and he initiated the set in 1921 with *The Golden Galleon* (F.114), a depiction of a Spanish galleon. Arms only created seven plates, including depictions of a junk, clipper ship, and small two-masted sailing ship, as illustrated by the Academy's impression of *Brig "Oleander,"* 1923 (F.131, pl. 10). However, as Arms later commented, "the fascination which the straight etched line, with its accompanying interpretation in black and white, exerts upon its devotees reclaimed me entirely…and I went back to it wholeheartedly."[45]

Figure 24
Arthur Wesley Dow,
1857–1922,
United States
Page from
Composition, 13th
edition, 1929

Arms' sustained efforts in aquatint were unprecedented at the time since no other American artist used the technique with such skill or frequency. The early years of the twentieth century witnessed artists exploring the potential of etching, drypoint, lithography, and woodcuts, but few adopted aquatinting. Although Winslow Homer incorporated it into his printmaking at the end of the nineteenth century, he only published eight prints and was not a major force in aquatint's introduction into the American printmaking vocabulary. Joseph Pennell, Charles Mielatz, and Arthur B. Davies also experimented with the process. Mielatz used it in cityscapes (fig. 23); Davies incorporated it into figurative prints such as *Maenads*, 1920 (fig. 25) where it contributed to their personal and evocative mood. Arms recognized his position as one of the few exponents of the process and stated that it "is little understood and practiced today and is in great need of redevelopment."[46]

Why did Arms reject aquatint and return "wholeheartedly" to etching? Why did he abandon mezzotint, drypoint, and lithography? Although it is to be expected that a developing artist would eagerly experiment in a variety of media during the early years of an advancing career, it is unclear why Arms decided to restrict himself exclusively to etching and not pursue his work in additional graphic media. With an artist who is willing to spend up to 2,000 hours creating an etching, it seems unlikely that the time it takes to pit a mezzotint plate would have been of concern to Arms. Perhaps since the artists with whom Arms felt the greatest affinity (printmakers such as Rembrandt, Whistler, and Meryon) expressed themselves primarily through etching, Arms naturally gravitated to that process. The overall softness of a mezzotinted or aquatinted image, the unsuitability of these processes to the exacting detail work toward which, as we shall see, Arms was slowly working may have been a factor in his decision not to create more. Perhaps most importantly, his decision to forsake the other media, especially the very tonal, non-linear processes of aquatint and mezzotint, relates to the subjective issue of aesthetics and Arms' concept of beauty. At the end of his career, in a letter to the print-maker Harry Newman Wickey, Arms succinctly commented on his approach to art and expressed his commitment to drawing: "I worship drawing and, next to feeling, place it above all else in pictorial and plastic art."[47] For Arms the draftsman, line etching was probably not only the obvious, but perhaps the only viable vehicle for his continuing artistic expression.

When Arms gave up aquatinting, he also abandoned the subjects and compositional format associated in his *oeuvre* with the process—sailboats, military craft, birds, flowers—and which connect his work so closely with Japanese prints. It is probable that Arms selected the soft tonal range of aquatint for his Japonesque images because it mimics so successfully the qualities found in Japanese woodblock prints. When he dropped aquatint for etching around 1920, it may have seemed appropriate to put away his thoughts of *ukiyo-e*-style compositions and subjects. Whatever the reason, Arms devoted the remainder of his career to etching, primarily putting needle to plate in architectural subjects.

1. Deborah J. Johnson, *Whistler to Weidenaar, American Prints 1870–1950, Gifts from the Fazzano Brothers and Other Donors*, exh. cat. (Providence: Museum of Art, Rhode Island School of Design, 1987), p. 10 and James Watrous, *A Century of American Printmaking, 1880–1980* (Madison, WI: The University of Wisconsin Press, 1984), p. 9.

2. Watrous, *A Century of American Printmaking*, pp. 3–20.

3. *Ibid.*, p. 28.

4. Richard S. Field, "Introduction to A Study of American Prints 1900–1950," in *American Prints 1900–1950*, exh. cat. (New Haven: Yale University Art Gallery, 1983), p. 19.

5. Watrous, *A Century of American Printmaking*, p. 32.

6. *Ibid.*, p. 31.

7. Arms and Arms, "Descriptive Catalogue," plate no. 1.

8. John Taylor Arms, "John Taylor Arms," in The Crafton Collection, comp. *John Taylor Arms*, vol. V of *American Etchers* (New York: The Crafton Collection, Inc., 1930), [pp. 3–4].

9. Although autobiographical statements such as the one just quoted allude to early visits to Europe, specific records detailing the where and when of the trips are unknown, unlocated, and unpublished. The pre-1923 prints themselves suggest the towns Arms visited, such as Rouen, Lisieux, Bayeux, Honfleur, etc.

10. Watrous, *A Century of American Printmaking*, p. 31.

11. Zigrosser, "The Artist in America," p. 25.

12. John Taylor Arms, *Handbook of Print Making and Print Makers* (New York: The Macmillan Company, 1934), pp. 18, 27.

13. John Taylor Arms, *Exhibition of Drawings, Including Work in Yucatan and Mexico and Etchings by John Taylor Arms, N.A., P.S.A.E., A.R.E.*, exh. invitation and brochure (New York: Kennedy & Company, 1942), [p. 3].

14. Arms, *Handbook*, p. 28.

15. *Ibid.*, p. 19.

16. *Ibid.*, p. 19.

17. *Ibid.*, p. 28.

18. S. William Pelletier, "John Taylor Arms, His World and Work," *Georgia Museum of Art Bulletin* 17 (1993), p. 5.

19. Katharine A. Lochnan, *The Etchings of James McNeill Whistler*, exh. cat. (New Haven and London: Yale University Press in association with the Art Gallery of Ontario, Toronto, 1984), pp. 85, 87.

20. Whistler's gravitation to this type of spatial construction likely results from his study of Pieter de Hooch, the seventeenth-century master of Dutch genre subjects. See Lochnan, *The Etchings of James McNeill Whistler*, p. 85.

21. Arms, *Handbook*, p. 28.

22. See *St. Albans (Sketch)*, 1922 (F.129); *Street in Borgio*, 1926 (F.179); *Old Rouen*, 1927 (F.203); and *Southover, Sussex "To F.L.M.G." (Sketch)*, 1942 (F.372), among others.

23. Lochnan, *The Etchings of James McNeill Whistler*, p. 53.

24. Fletcher, *John Taylor Arms, A Man for All Time*, p. 15.

25. For example, the sheet Arms used for the Academy's impression of *Sunlight and Shadow* (fig. 3) has gilded edges; that for *Abside de la Cathédrale de Saint Pierre et Saint Paul, Troyes* (pl. 3) seems to be from an old ledger.

26. Fletcher, *John Taylor Arms, A Man for All Time*, p. 15.

27. John Taylor Arms, "John Taylor Arms Tells How He Makes an Etching, Part 3—Printing," *American Artist* 5, no. 2 (Feb. 1941), p. 13.

28. 4/75 (HAA 20,483) is printed on an off-white sheet; 5/75 (HAA 6526) appears on a cream sheet.

29. Arms, *Handbook*, p. 10.

30. *Ibid.*, p. 11.

31. *Ibid.*, p. 22.

32. Arms and Arms, "Descriptive Catalogue," plate no. 12. *A Souvenir*, 1919 (F.38) is Arms' second drypoint.

33. *Ibid.*, plate no. 67.

34. Kropfl, "A Catalogue of the Work of John Taylor Arms," p. 16.

35. Arms and Arms, "Descriptive Catalogue," plate no. 50.

36. The term *"shin hanga,"* or "new print," refers to the revival of Japanese woodblock printing during the first decades of the twentieth century.

37. Cynthia Eaton, "The Aquatints of John Taylor Arms," *The Print Connoisseur* 1, no. 2 (Dec. 1920), p. 110.

38. Julia Meech, "Collecting Japanese Art in America," in *Japonisme Comes to America, The Japanese Impact on the Graphic Arts, 1876–1925*, exh. cat. (New York: Harry N. Abrams, Inc., in association with The Jane Voorhees Zimmerli Art Museum, Rutgers, The State University of New Jersey, 1990), p. 43.

39. Lochnan, *The Etchings of James McNeill Whistler*, p. 94.

40. Julia Meech, "Japonisme: Graphic Arts in the Early Twentieth Century," in *The New Wave, Twentieth-Century Japanese Prints from the Robert O. Muller Collection* (London: Bamboo Publishing Ltd. in association with Hotei Japanese prints, Leiden, 1993), p. 41.

41. Julia Meech, "Reinventing the Exotic Orient," in *Japonisme Comes to America, The Japanese Impact on the Graphic Arts, 1876–1925*, p. 139.

42. *Ibid.*, p. 139.

43. Arthur Wesley Dow, *Composition*, 13th edition (Garden City, New York: Doubleday, Doran & Company, Inc., 1929), p. 7.

44. Cynthia Eaton, *John Taylor Arms, Aquatinter* (Boston: Charles E. Goodspeed & Co., 1923), p. 18.

45. Pelletier, "John Taylor Arms, His World and Work," p. 10.

46. *Ibid.*, p. 10.

47. Letter from John Taylor Arms to Harry Newman Wickey, dated Fairfield, CT, Jan. 18, 1947 (Harry Wickey Papers, 3683:259, AAA). Arms repeated the same sentiment in correspondence with other individuals such as Leon Kroll and Barry Faulkner. See letter from John Taylor Arms to Leon Kroll, dated North Pomfret, VT, Sept. 13, 1949 (Leon Kroll Papers, D326:24, AAA) and letter from Arms to Barry Faulkner, dated Fairfield, CT, Mar. 10, 1953 (Leon Kroll Papers, D326:32, AAA).

Plate 1
A Roof in Thiers,
1921
Etching on green
paper
6³⁄₈ x 3¹⁄₈ in.
(16.2 x 7.9 cm)
Gift of Richard H.
and Helen T.
Hagemeyer, 1989
(20,635)

Plate 2
La Tour d'Horloge,
Dinan, 1932
Etching on
green paper
9³⁄₈ x 4 in.
(23.8 x 10.2 cm)
Gift of Richard H.
and Helen T.
Hagemeyer, 1988
(20,489)

Plate 4
Stockholm, 1940
Etching, aquatint
on green paper
7¹¹⁄₁₆ x 13⅝ in.
(19.5 x 34.6 cm)
Purchase, 1941
(11,812)

Plate 5
Crystal and Jade,
1936–40
Etching, aquatint
on green paper
7½ x 6¹¹⁄₁₆ in.
(19.1 x 17.0 cm)
Purchase, C.
Montague Cooke, Jr.
Fund, 1993 (24,082)

Plate 6
Moonlight, Rangeley Lake, 1920
Mezzotint printed in green ink
7¹⁵⁄₁₆ x 4⅞ in.
(20.2 x 12.4 cm)
Purchase, C. Montague Cook, Jr. Fund, 1993 (24,079)

Plate 7
"S.C.'s" On Night Patrol, 1920
Etching, aquatint printed in blue ink
3⅞ x 10 in.
(9.8 x 25.4 cm)
Gift of Richard H. and Helen T. Hagemeyer, 1989 (20,613)

Plate 8
Moonlight, Number One, 1920
Etching, aquatint printed in blue ink
7³⁄₈ x 2³⁄₈ in.
(18.7 x 6.0 cm)
Gift of Richard H. and Helen T. Hagemeyer, 1993
(24,030)

Plate 9
Isola Bella, Lake Maggiore, 1920
Etching, aquatint printed in color
$5^{15}/_{16}$ x $13^5/_8$ in.
(15.1 x 34.6 cm)
Purchase, C. Montague Cooke, Jr. Fund, 1993 (24,078)

Plate 10
Brig "Oleander," 1923
Etching, aquatint printed in color
$8^5/_8$ x $10^1/_8$ in.
(21.9 x 25.7 cm)
Gift of Richard H. and Helen T. Hagemeyer, 1990 (20,816)

Honolulu Academy of Arts   39

Plate 11
Out of My Window,
1916
Etching printed with
chine collé
7⅞ x 6 in.
(20.0 x 15.2 cm)
Gift of Eliza Lefferts
and Charles
Montague Cooke,
Jr., 1941 (11,697)

John Taylor Arms

American Gothic:
The New York Series

After first picking up his needle in 1913/14, Arms made rapid progress in mastering the complexities of intaglio printmaking, especially etching and aquatint. The fourteen plates in Arms' *New York Series*, created concurrently with many of his aquatints, European gable and street scenes, and prints in the *Maine Series*, provide an interesting overview of the artist's advancement from early efforts to mature vision. The Academy is fortunate to possess impressions of the majority of the significant prints in this series, allowing an in-depth consideration of their importance and place in the context of Arms' career and American architectural printmaking.

Printed views of American architectural subjects have a lengthy history in American graphic arts. City views date back to the seventeenth century with renderings of New York City, or as it was then known, New Amsterdam.[1] City views increased and diversified during the eighteenth century, as printmakers depicted historical events. Paul Revere recorded the confrontation of British and colonial troops in Boston's King Street in 1770; Amos Doolittle engraved George Washington's inauguration at New York's Federal Hall in 1790.[2] The growth of American urban areas during the first half of the nineteenth century together with increased prosperity and a sense of pride of place spurred printmakers to engrave views of cities from north to south and east to west, including Buffalo, Philadelphia, and Richmond.[3] The publication of wood engravings in books, magazines, and, most especially, weeklies such as *Harper's Weekly* continued the dissemination of printed urban and architectural subjects.[4]

As mentioned in the previous chapter, American and European architectural themes entered into American fine-art printmaking as Joseph Pennell, Charles Mielatz, and other leaders of the etching revival published prints during the second half of the nineteenth century and first half of the twentieth. Charles Mielatz is generally regarded as the first major printmaker to devote a significant body of work to the depiction of New York City, creating strikingly composed images of sites such as Washington Arch, Madison Square, and docks on the East River (fig. 23).[5] Pennell complemented his early picturesque scenes of Old World Europe with dramatic views of American and European industrialization dating from as early as 1905.[6] For instance, powerfully composed and evocative images document the construction of the Panama Canal, the massive industrial complexes in Belgium and Germany, and the skyscrapers of New York City. Rendering a view of New York City in *Out of My Window* (F.4, pl. 11) in 1916, Arms joined the ranks of printmakers fascinated by the city. With all but one of the plates of his *New York Series* dating from 1916 to 1922, Arms was a contemporary of John Marin and Childe Hassam and should be considered a forerunner of New York City's other most famous architectural celebrants of the twentieth century, Charles Sheeler, Howard Cook, and Louis Lozowick, among others (fig. 28). Indeed, Arms was one of the first twentieth-century artists to create a significant body of work devoted to this symbol of progress and modernity.

Figure 26
*West Forty-Second
Street*, 1920
Etching
13⅛ x 10½ in.
(33.3 x 26.7 cm)
Purchase, Academy
Volunteers Fund,
1989 (20,545)

Arms' first depictions of New York follow the pictorial tradition of recording architectural monuments first established by Pennell and Mielatz. As the descriptive title suggests, *Out of My Window* (F.4, pl. 11) presents the view Arms enjoyed from the office he had with his partner Cameron Clark. The tower of the Woolworth Building is faintly visible as it soars behind the shadowed lowrise structure in the foreground. Arms, still mastering the process of multiple bitings in this his fourth published work, seems to have simply stopped out the background, or upper half of the plate, and continued etching the darker foreground or lower half of the image; plate tone across the lowrise takes care of the rest of the shadowy illusion.

The Academy's impression of *Out of My Window* reveals another level of Arms' early experimentation. It is one of two works in the collection printed with *chine collé*, a

Figure 27
Cobwebs, 1921
Etching
9⅝ x 7½ in.
(24.4 x 19.1 cm)
Purchase, Academy
Volunteers Fund,
1993 (24,094)

delicate piece of tissue the size of the print's plate mounted on a larger, heavier sheet of paper before printing.[7] Although the *chine collé* adds richness to the print's inking and depth to the sense of the printed image on the sheet, Arms' interest in the process apparently was not fixed. Only rarely did he adopt this process during his career.

Arms' *New York Series* spans the two years the artist devoted so much energy to aquatint: 1919 and 1920. *The Sarah Jane, New York*, 1920 (F. 56, pl. 12), created with etching and aquatint, represents an interesting extension of Arms' Japonesque compositions of becalmed sailboats. In this image infused with nostalgia, Arms ignored the rapid pulse of life in twentieth-century New York City and took a moment to enjoy the leisurely passage of the *Sarah Jane*, an old-fashioned river sloop, in front of Manhattan's dramatic and modern skyline. With its sense of movement, humanity, specificity of location, and detail, this print does not seem to have much in common with *Moonlight, Number One* (pl. 8) beyond a superficiality of subject. Nonetheless, the abrupt truncation of the mast as a compositional device, the pictorial tension between the mast and horizon, and that between the vessel's stern and the plate's edge suggest Arms' consideration of Japanese design aesthetics as he sought his own artistic vision (fig. 21).

In another work of 1920, *West Forty-Second Street* (F.41, fig. 26), Arms turned to the city's energy, growth, and modernity. The print depicts a view from Fifth Avenue along West Forty-Second Street towards the station of the Sixth Avenue elevated train (now demolished); the New York Public Library is at left. In most of Arms' prints, the human figure is absent or it appears as a picturesque element in the medieval quarters of European towns or the Maine woodlands (figs. 11–12). Here, however, Arms captured the hustle and flow of urban life as crowds and traffic throng the thoroughfare. In commenting on the energy and movement which infuse a comparable subject created in 1916 by Childe Hassam, a depiction of Fifth Avenue at Thirty-Fourth Street, it is as if Arms is articulating his thoughts on his own *West Forty-Second Street*:

> *It is a matter of pattern, but of one evoked by soaring architectural forms. And even as the light plays over their surfaces and around their corners (note the significance in the introduction into the design of the great white pier at the left), so do the tiny human figures, the cabs, and the buses, move through the print, creating motion in the tangible as well as the intangible elements portrayed.*[8]

The exaggerated perspective of the library and other buildings lining West Forty-Second Street intensify the sense of incessant movement that Arms discovered in New York and celebrated in this print. As previously discussed, Arms derived this type of compositional format from his consideration of Whistler's prints and entered it into his own vocabulary (fig. 7).

Arms again turned to Whistler for inspiration in the creation of *Cobwebs*, 1921 (F.95, fig. 27), the first of his two views of the Brooklyn Bridge, a subject which preoccupied many later etchers of New York architectural subjects including Louis Lozowick (fig. 28). In this picturesque image of lower Manhattan, Arms effectively captured the texture, tone, and details of the brick buildings, paved street, bridge towers, and spider-like cables, the delicate geometric patterning of the latter suggesting the title of the print. The startlingly bold truncation of the man in the lower left corner derives from a comparable device in Whistler's *Rotherhithe* of 1860 (fig. 29), another print of a working-class community linked by location to river traffic and trade. *Rotherhithe*, one of the twelve plates that comprise Whistler's *Thames Set*, is also one of his best-known early works. Arms paid further homage to Whistler by incorporating much of the print's basic compositional format into his own etching. Like Whistler, he divided his view into off-center vertical units, with sharply skewed facades on the right. He also framed the view of the distant river, in this case with the span of the Brooklyn Bridge instead of an architectural cross beam. Arms' understanding of Whistler's compositional innovations is an important component in the mastery of forceful design which characterizes much of his printmaking from this point onward.

Arms' second depiction of the Brooklyn Bridge, *The Gates of the City*, 1922 (F.126, pl. 13), approaches the monument of modern engineering from an entirely different perspective. Unlike the distant view presented in *Cobwebs*, in this work Arms delineated one

tower which, articulated by two pointed arches, is powerful in its symmetry and frontality. The incredible delicacy of tone and exacting representation of each brick and twist of the cables testify to Arms' technical virtuosity. The Brooklyn Bridge may have represented for Arms a synthesis of symbol and spirituality encompassing the truth and majesty of medieval architecture and the beauty and modernity of New York. Arms devoted the majority of his work after 1922 to depictions of Gothic architecture which, he once wrote, was "imbued, from foundations to loftiest pinnacle, with [a] spirit of medieval devotion and aspirational exuberance."[9] Not only did Arms believe that Gothic architecture embodies man's greatest achievement, here, stylistically, it underlies an engineering wonder and traditional emblem of the city. *The Gates of the City*, integrating Arms' technical brilliance, compositional boldness, and conceptual depth, is one of his finest prints.

In 1913, President Woodrow Wilson opened New York's Woolworth Building, the highest structure in the world until 1931. The building is readily identifiable in several of Arms' prints, including *Out of My Window* (pl. 11) and *An American Cathedral*, 1921 (F.107, pl. 14). The Woolworth Building and the Brooklyn Bridge were glorious symbols of modern architecture and popular subjects in American art during the first decades of the twentieth century. To many American artists, structures such as the Woolworth Building represented the triumph of technology and the growth of the United States' urban environment. Charles Sheeler, Howard Cook, Louis Lozowick, and Armin Landeck among others emphasized the grandeur of buildings such as it in their printmaking, just as Georgia O'Keeffe eulogized the Shelton and Radiator Buildings in her painting. To Arms, however, the Woolworth Building, with its elaborately ornamented spires and delicately arched arcades, was also a modern expression of Gothic architectural principles. Arms emphasized its soaring height with the strongly vertical shape of the plate, as well as by selecting a low vantage point for the view, presenting it from between two shadowed columns, and showing it towering over City Hall. Arms elaborated the Gothic architectural motifs of the building with careful detail and strongly etched work; he also bathed the scene in a dramatic play of light and shade, including the radiation of an almost divine

light from above. The title of the print—*An American Cathedral*—clinches the structure's passage from an earthly existence into the spiritual realm of Gothic architecture.

An American Cathedral and *The Gates of the City* presage Arms' commitment during the 1920s to Gothic architecture in Europe. New York held no interest for Arms after 1922, although he etched one more plate in 1935 for the *New York Series, From Knoedler's Window, MCMXXXV*, 1935 (F.293). Arms explained this change of mind in his statement of 1930, "As for my own land, I can admire the skyscrapers of New York, that unbelievable city which is a very gold mine for the architectural etcher, but I cannot love them and I cannot etch what I do not love."[10] Indeed, Arms professed discomfort with the modern world. He rejected new conveniences such as radio and telephone, and he remained largely unmoved by contemporary architecture founded on technological advancements.[11] Instead, he discovered an affirmation of life and spirituality in the Gothic era. His profound affinity for the "medieval devotion and aspirational exuberance" of Gothic architecture reflects his belief that Gothic structures were tangible evidence of the spiritual life of the period:

> *[Gothic monuments] were born of an age when man's need for the expression of his spiritual ideals drove him to heights of architectural conception and execution to which he has never since attained.... These emblems of man's faith and hope soar skyward, pointing their glorious towers to the heaven which inspired their erection.*[12]

He consciously strove to infuse his etching with a Gothic spirituality "which is as far removed as possible from the materialism and regimentation of today."[13] So it was that from 1923 to the end of his career, Arms devoted the majority of his major printmaking efforts to European Gothic architectural subjects. The irony of this narrowing of focus is that Arms' *New York Series*, a series which the artist decided not to further develop, includes some of the most innovative and progressive works of his career.

1. Frank Weitenkampf, "American City Views in American Prints," *The Print Connoisseur* 5 (Jan. 1925), p. 25.
2. *Ibid.*, 26.
3. *Ibid.*, pp. 29–30.
4. *Ibid.*, p. 32.
5. Johnson, *Whistler to Weidenaar, American Prints 1870–1950*, p. 14.
6. Watrous, *A Century of American Printmaking*, pp. 36–37.
7. The other work in the Academy's collection printed with chine collé also dates from Arms' early experimental years—*Veterans*, 1916 (F.6).
8. John Taylor Arms, "Childe Hassam, Etcher of Light," *Prints* 4, no. 1 (Nov. 1933), p. 10.
9. John Taylor Arms, "Gothic A.D. 1941," *Carnegie Magazine* 19, no. 10 (Apr. 1946), p. 290.
10. Arms, "John Taylor Arms," [p. 6].
11. Bassham, *John Taylor Arms*, p. 6.
12. Arms, "John Taylor Arms," [p. 5].
13. Arms, "Gothic A.D. 1941," p. 290.

The Search for Truth and Beauty:
Arms' European Architectural Subjects

A deeply religious man, Arms sought a means of expressing his spiritual ideals, his belief in the uplifting power of truth and beauty; he recognized depictions of Gothic structures as his vehicle. As articulate with words as he was with plate and needle, Arms disclosed the most fundamental premises of his printmaking in a number of published statements. Arms explained his recognition of the physical perfection in Gothic structures, the spiritual purity with which they were conceived and constructed, and their ability to inspire finer feelings. He wrote that in the cathedrals and churches constructed during the Gothic era:

> *truth and beauty have flowered as, to me, in no other monuments erected by the hand of man. They were born of an age when man's need for the expression of his spiritual ideals drove him to heights of architectural conception and execution to which he has never since attained.*[1]

Arms elaborated on the spiritual commitment of the individuals who designed and built them in another statement:

> *The devotion and aspiration that went into their construction is echoed in every line and detail and mass. From the architects who planned them down to the humblest stonecutter who carved the most inconspicuous of their mouldings, we feel a spiritual and imaginative fervor which has no parallel in the history of building.*[2]

He described their subjugation of self in the cause of a higher purpose:

> *These architects, builders, and artisans, gave their all that their churches might be worthy. Some were, at best, but lesser craftsmen, as some were of the greatest, but all were animated by the same motive—the sense of spiritual dedication which counted time as naught so long as the end was attained.*[3]

Arms identified himself as a "mediævalist" who, striving to express divine beauty, responded to "an impulse akin to that of the builders of old when they gave unstintingly of their love and labor as a votive offering in the accomplishment of a purpose which

Figure 30
Guardians of the Spire, 1921
Etching
6⅝ x 9⅞ in.
(16.8 x 25.1 cm)
Gift of Lila L. and James F. Morgan, 1983 (18,567)

transcended any consideration of individual fame—the creation of the Gothic church."[4] Arms' prints of Gothic structures represent his "deepest sense of beauty in the effort to recreate the glory which, though of another age, endures throughout the centuries."[5] Arms gave of himself to invite in others the experience of divine truth and beauty that he recognized in the soaring spires, flying buttresses, and delicate ornamentation of Gothic structures.

Arms was not the first to search for a bygone era that could express the aspirations of the day. Although revivals of cultural heritage began as early as the Renaissance with its rebirth of the ideals of classical antiquity, they frequently recurred during the 1700s and 1800s in both Europe and the United States; they reached a period of vibrant fulfillment in the last half of the nineteenth century. The publication of three books between 1851 and 1868 were instrumental in establishing the influence of Gothic art for the remainder of the century: John Ruskin's *The Stones of Venice* (1851–53); Bruce J. Talbert's *Gothic Forms Applied to Furniture, Metal Work, and Decoration for Domestic Purposes* (1867), and finally in 1868 Charles Locke Eastlake's *Hints on Household Taste in Furniture, Upholstery, and Other Details*. Eastlake, a proponent of medieval spirit and principles, continued to enjoy remarkable influence in the United States decades after the publication of his guide.[6] The Gothic Revival affected almost every American art form at that time, including painting, printmaking, the decorative arts, and architecture.[7]

Ralph Adams Cram, an American architect and writer active around the turn of the century, also vigorously supported the recognition of Gothic architecture as one of spirituality, honest design, and fine craftsmanship.[8] In an era marked by increased modernization and urban growth, Cram celebrated pre-industrial values such as honesty, truth, and beauty through his endorsement of Gothic architecture. Arms' depictions of the glorious monuments of Gothic architecture and his wish to evoke the spirit of the era did not appear in a vacuum. They represent a late flowering of the Gothic Revival in the United States and a nostalgia for a simpler, truer age.

Arms' interest in Gothic ecclesiastical architecture first appeared in his etchings of 1920. He did not render the facade of a Gothic church or cathedral as would have logically followed his concurrent work—the picturesque views of medieval house fronts in the *Gable Series*. Instead, he devoted two plates to the depiction of gargoyles and elaborated on the theme ten more times before the end of 1924.[9] The Academy's

collection numbers impressions of four prints in the series, including the finely detailed miniature print, *A Gargoyle, Lincoln Cathedral*, 1920 (F.92), and two of the best-known images in the series, *Guardians of the Spire*, 1921 (F.102, fig. 30) and *Le Penseur de Notre Dame*, 1923 (F.136, fig. 31).

Gargoyles, dating from as early as Greek and Roman times, are decorative spouts in the form of imaginary figures (animal or human) which drain rain water from roof gutters. Bypassing the Romanesque architectural vocabulary of the eleventh and twelfth centuries, they achieved full expression in the Gothic cathedrals of England and Europe. Medieval designers and stonecutters at times ignored the functional aspect of the gargoyles and allowed the otherworldly creatures to serve purely ornamental, sculptural ends. The spirited animation and fantastic imaginative qualities of the gargoyles attracted Arms' consideration. He stated that the *Gargoyle Series* gave him "endless pleasure" in its devotion:

> to those queer, grim grotesques, often humorous, sometimes tragic
> and always entirely fascinating, which constitute such telling
> decorative accents on all the great Gothic buildings of France.
> Magnificent in design and beautiful in execution, they are
> a never-ending source of interest to the student of mediæval
> architecture and a never-failing temptation to the pencil
> of the draughtsman.[10]

Arms captured the lively character of gargoyles on different cathedrals, including those in Lincoln, Rheims, and Amboise, but his most complex compositions are animated by the mystical beings hovering over the cities of Amiens and Paris. Perched high above the city in *Guardians of the Spire,* a winged and a wingless gargoyle stretch their necks and eagerly peer down on the city faintly etched in below them. One of the most famous gargoyles of Paris' Notre Dame appears in *Le Penseur de Notre Dame*; Le Stryge rests its elbows on the balustrade with chin in hands while gazing resignedly over the city.[11]

The gargoyles of Notre Dame and the cathedral in Amiens attracted the attention of several printmakers before Arms. In 1911 the British etcher David Young Cameron published the same view of the same two gargoyles at Amiens (fig. 32), providing at the very least a direct precedent for Arms' *Guardians of the Spire,* if not actual inspiration. Charles Meryon and Joseph Pennell worked from the same vantage point as did Arms in their representations of Le Stryge, published in 1853 and 1893, respectively.[12]

More than mere imitation, the *Gargoyle Series* represents a new level of draftsmanship, technical refinement, and sophistication of concept beyond what Arms had achieved in his earlier work. Arms restrained the loose, agile linework notable in the *Maine Series* and used instead the sharp point of his needle and tightly meshed marks to work his compositions across the entire plate. He carefully built up each image with extraordinary detail, rich modeling, and fine textures; note in the prints illustrated here the very tactile, pitted, weather-worn quality of the stone that serves both as supple body and crumbling structure. Furthermore, in rendering the tonal qualities of these prints, Arms eschewed the aquatint process with which he was so familiar. A careful examination of *Le Penseur de Notre Dame,* especially when aided by magnification, reveals the squiggles, contours, dots, patchwork pattern of dense hatching, and other marks through which Arms delineated the creature. The patchwork

Figure 32
David Young Cameron, 1865–1945, England
The Wingless Chimera, 1911
Etching
7⅝ x 9⁷⁄₁₆ in.
(19.4 x 24 cm)
Honolulu Academy of Arts
Gift of Mrs. J. B. Guard, 1962
(14,832)

hatching, so important here to the representation of the stone and the sense of time's passage, became an important tool for Arms in his later work as he became increasingly concerned with the very precise definition of shape, volume, and texture.[13]

Arms' *Gargoyle Series* also reveals his deep interest in expressing what he perceived to be the spirit of the subjects and their physical appearance. For Arms, the stone fabric of the Gothic structures he so admired was not inanimate; it was vibrant and alive. Arms indicated that it was this vital quality that he generally found in the work of Meryon and which he hoped to infuse in his own:

> *Everywhere it is the essential spirit I have sought to express, rather than the literal outward aspect....For as a building possesses, as truly as does a human being, a skeleton, a covering of flesh, and clothing with which both are in turn covered, so also, and most poignantly, does it possess a spirit. In the work of the great inter-preters of architecture in terms of line—men like Meryon, Piranesi, Canaletto, and Bone—it is this expression of the spirit of the subject, and not its mere physical appearance, which makes them such enduring works of art.*[14]

Indeed, approaching their characterization with sympathetic whimsy and humor, Arms developed the uncanny ability to infuse these fantastic stone beings with an animate sense of life. Undoubtedly part of the inanimate stone fabric of the architectural

Figure 33
Puerta del Obispo, Zamora, 1933
Etching
12⅝ x 7¼ in.
(32.1 x 18.4 cm)
Gift of Richard H. and Helen T. Hagemeyer, 1990
(20,861)

Figure 34
Stone Tapestry, San Isidoro, León, 1933
Etching
11⅝ x 3¹/₁₆ in.
(29.5 x 7.8 cm)
Gift of Richard H. and Helen T. Hagemeyer, 1990
(20,862)

monument, the gargoyles in *Guardians of the Spire* nonetheless are filled with curiosity and strain to keep track of the activities taking place under their aeries. Although motionless, Le Stryge is hardly grim or forboding; the creature wistfully contemplates its view of Paris. Lightly etched, the city is subordinate to the gargoyle and is an effective foil to its appealing expression of resignation as it faces its eternal vigil over the city. The gargoyles into which Arms breathed life personify the enduring spirituality that the artist hoped to infuse into the representations of Gothic architecture which preoccupied so much of his attention throughout the remainder of his career.

Arms' sustained fascination with Gothic architecture runs through the prints he published beginning in 1923 and which he divided into designated groups—the *Spanish Church Series*, *French Church Series*, *English Series*, and *Italian Series*. The *Spanish Church Series* and *French Church Series* started to take shape in 1923 and 1924, respectively. Numbering fifty-five major works, the *French Church Series* is Arms' most complex suite of related plates. The beginning of the *Italian Series* followed immediately the preceding two when it recorded the first of its twenty-seven plates in 1925. In addition to being published in edition form, many of the French and Italian subjects were reproduced in the two travel books Arms produced in collaboration with his wife. *Churches of France* came out in 1929, and *Hill Towns and Cities of Northern Italy* appeared in 1932.[15] Arms etched the first of the fifteen rural scenes of Hertfordshire, Berkshire, and Buckinghamshire that constitute the *English Series* several years later in 1937. Within the narrow range of Gothic architecture, the prints that underlie these series represent a broad spectrum of subjects and reveal Arms' stylistic and conceptual development.

Although many of the prints in Arms' various series present general views of different cities and towns, Le Puy, Rocamadour, Finchingfield, etc., his vision is most powerfully expressed in representations of the glorious cathedrals and churches of Spain and France. While working on his *Gargoyle Series*, Arms etched the first plates in his *Spanish Church Series*, which was begun during a driving and sketching tour of Europe with his wife Dorothy. Generally spending a few days in each location, Arms first searched out and then carefully drew his views for later reference in the creation of a print.

The exact subjects of his plates depended on what struck him most about the structure he wished to depict. At times he focused on large details, such as in the oblique presentation of the Bishop's Door in *Puerta del Obispo, Zamora*, 1933 (F.266, fig. 33), or on smaller details such as in the skewed view of a fragment of a portal in *Stone Tapestry, San Isidoro, León*, 1933 (F.267, fig. 34). The strikingly narrow format and exaggerated perspective of the basilica's south portal as well as the virtuoso rendering of form, detail, texture, and pattern of light and shade make the print one of Arms' most elegant. Unlike *Sunlight and Shadow* (fig. 3), Arms' first published print and one in which he did not remember to reverse the lettering of a sign before printing, the inscription on this print is exquisite in its beauty and clarity, especially given the additional complexity of seemingly being "engraved" on stone. That Arms' control of the etching process was remarkable is widely recognized; it has also tended to overshadow general awareness of his keen sense of composition and design. Prints such as *Stone Tapestry* and *Puerta del Obispo*, daring in their raking perspectives and massing of forms, bear witness to Arms' willingness to challenge pictorial convention with prints that are exciting and powerful in form.

Arms often stepped back, considered the structure in its entirety, and selected a view which was compositionally sound and best presented the monument in its Gothic glory. As he discovered during his European tours, however, cities and towns had grown up around the structures of greatest interest to him, making it difficult to identify his best perspective. Arms first scouted out the view he wished to delineate and then set to work with paper, pencil, and drafting board to sketch the image. Depending on the complexity of the print he planned to create and limitations set by the tour itinerary, Arms spent anywhere between a few hours to several days on a drawing that he later transferred to a plate and etched.[16] When in Seville, Arms sketched La Giralda, a twelfth-century mosque minaret later incorporated into the city's cathedral, for *"La Giralda," Seville*, 1924 (F.145, fig. 35), the fourth of the fifteen plates in the *Spanish Church Series*. Diary entries dating from Arms' visit to the city provide insights into his thoughts on the beauty of the subject and the trials of sketching the tower over a three-day period. After his first day in Seville, Arms wrote:

> *The cathedral is enormous—the biggest Gothic church in the world and second only to St. Peters in size among all churches. The exterior is, however, hard to see and not as interesting as Burgos. Tramped all over the town with D[orothy] but could not settle on anything. Will try the roof of the American consulate to-morrow morning. La Giralda (model for tower of Madison Square Garden) [is] the most beautiful tower I have seen in Spain. It is the chief feature of the exterior of the cathedral and is—to me—as perfect as architecture can be. Proportions and silhouette flawless and detail rich, well placed and perfect in scale.[17]*

The following day Arms resumed his search for the most satisfactory view and, thanks to the cooperation of the American consulate, found it:

Figure 35
"La Giralda,"
Seville, 1924
Etching
$12^{5}/_{16}$ x $7^{3}/_{4}$ in.
(31.3 x 19.7 cm)
Gift of Richard H.
and Helen T.
Hagemeyer, 1990
(20,819)

Up early and went to look for view of cathedral before breakfast. Crossed the river but found nothing. After breakfast went to American consulate, was shown to roof and decided to draw La Giralda. American consul...and Vice Consul...very obliging and thoughtful men....At work till nearly seven, when light gave out.[18]

Arms finished the drawing on the third day, working until four in the afternoon, but making sure to take time out for lunch![19]

Given the courtesy of the American consulate and privacy of his lookout, the sketching of La Giralda must have been one of Arms' easier ventures. On other trips to Spain, Arms was pestered by hoards of spectators and bothersome children.[20] Dorothy Arms described most vividly the challenges of being an artist working outdoors when Arms sketched his views, subject to the ceaseless bustle of passersby and the object of curiosity all around. When Arms drew the west facade of Rouen's cathedral of Notre Dame for *Lace in Stone, Rouen Cathedral*, 1927 (F.200), she wrote:

There simply was no sequestered nook, no half sheltered corner into which he might withdraw himself in partial seclusion; only a small pavement too narrow to hold the jostling crowds who used it, parallel tracks on which the trams passed each other at frequent intervals, an 'island of safety' perilously inadequate, and the open square into which came carriages and taxis, carts and great camions from four different directions....Four days of intensive work under the worst possible conditions succeeded. The passing traffic sent grit and choking dust on to the drawing and into eyes already half blinded by the glare, and heads cast black replicas of themselves which jerked confusingly across the white paper as their owners peered at it from different angles. People getting on and off the trams tripped over the knapsack and bumped against the stool in passing.[21]

Irrespective of the difficulty in selecting the best views, Arms recognized the pictorial potential of sites where contemporary reality confronts Gothic ecclesiastical structures, their enduring spirituality an immutable constant despite the changes of time. *"La Giralda," Seville* is one of many striking, related compositions in which his medieval subject—a Gothic cathedral or church facade, tower, nave, doorway, rose window, porch, or other portion of the structure—rises with majestic beauty above or beyond the aging medieval quarter of the city. In *"La Giralda," Seville* Arms juxtaposed the height and refined ornamental delicacy of the soaring tower with the here-and-now aspects of aging stucco and irregular rooflines, balconies, and windows of the houses clustered below. The image is also one of formal oppositions. Dots are in counterpoint to linework, light summary strokes to precise detail, silvery half-lights to shimmering shadows. With a sure hand, Arms contrasted areas of primary importance and fully worked detail with sketchily treated areas of less importance. He created a print in which its beauty and delicacy of expression match that of his subject. A similar compositional conception underlies many of the first prints in his *Spanish Church Series, French Church Series,* and *Italian Series* which date from 1923 to around 1928: *Bourges,* 1925 (F.166), *Mont Saint-Michel,* 1926 (F.182, fig. 36), *Rodez,* 1927 (F.189, pl. 15), and *"La Mangia," Siena,* 1927 (F.192).

Figure 36
Mont Saint-Michel,
1926
Etching
15³⁄₁₆ x 11¹¹⁄₁₆ in.
(38.6 x 29.7 cm)
Gift of Walter
Crandall, 1970
(16,192)

Arms published the first plate of the *French Church Series* in 1924, the year after his first Spanish image. Comprising fifty-five works, the series is one of the largest created during his career and includes prints detailing the churches and cathedrals at the heart of France's Gothic architectural heritage. He rendered the major structures of Paris, Chartres, Rouen, and Mont Saint-Michel, as well as those in more provincial communities such as Rodez, Troyes, and Pèrigueux. Although Arms rendered images of well-known towns and sites in Spain, Italy, and even Belgium, it was France that he "always most dearly loved to draw."[22]

The maturity of vision and technical sophistication at the heart of the *French Church Series* surpass the simplicity and quaintness of France's Old World street scenes with which Arms began his career. A comparison of *Mont Saint-Michel* and *Aspiration, La Madeleine, Verneuil-sur-Avre,* 1939 (F.329, fig. 37) illustrates the continuing development of Arms' work. Mont Saint-Michel is one of France's most beloved natural curiosities and architectural monuments. The Mont is an isolated cone of granite rising abruptly from the Gulf of Saint-Malo, around the base of which is built a medieval town. The mont is surmounted by its famous abbey church, notable for a profusion of delicately ornamented flying buttresses and pinnacles. As in *"La Giralda," Seville,* Arms removed himself from the abbey's actual site and selected a vantage point that allowed him to contrast the soaring towers and exquisite balance of mass, proportion, and decoration found in Gothic ecclesiastical structures with the charming vagaries of a community's everyday life—aging houses, sagging roofs, rambling vegetation, and open windows. Arms thus continued to introduce elements of the picturesque into his depictions of Gothic architecture. The careful drawing and details which articulate the houses and abbey give way to more summarily treated border areas. Loose linework and sketchy forms representing the wall, freestanding structure, and greenery at the base of the print reflect Arms' continuing interest in a personal and facile drawing style, as already noted in the *Maine Series,* and lend a sense of lightness and airiness to the image. However, despite its obvious ties to the artist's early efforts, the large scale, complexity of the composition, and skill with which it is etched testify to a new level of achievement.

After 1927/28, Arms narrowed his focus both formally and conceptually with his major French, Spanish, and Italian Gothic architectural themes. As in *Aspiration, La Madeleine, Verneuil-sur-Avre,* Arms generally allowed architectural subjects to stand alone as symbols of faith and beauty, free of the secular allusions and picturesque motifs represented by the towns encircling the foundations of the structures. The small town of Verneuil-sur-Avre, situated in the heart of Normandy between Rouen and Le Mans,

is known for La Madeleine, a Flamboyant Gothic tower with octagonal lantern (and adjacent Renaissance porch) which is so tall that it dwarfs the rest of the church. With superb draftsmanship, absolute precision of architectural detail, and careful massing of light and shade, Arms delineated the elevation of the tower and porch. Mass, volume, tonal nuance, and detail result from linework painstakingly and delicately etched across the entire surface of the plate. Each stone, sprocket, lacelike line of tracery, and statue adorning the tower appears in testimony to Arms' infinite patience in creating them out of linework so fine that much of it is visible only with magnification. Gone are the quaint house fronts and charming figures so important to the earlier prints; the picturesque, the agile, and the spontaneous no longer enjoy a role in Arms' expression of Gothic glory. Arms explained that in these prints he attempted to:

> *record mass and detail, textures and chiaroscuro, as I have seen*
> *them. I have not tried to express abstract ideas, or to 'suggest' what*
> *I felt and leave it to the observer of my prints to supply what I have*

omitted, but rather to state, in terms as lucid, comprehensive, and intelligible as lay within my power, exactly what moved me so deeply. Convinced that I could not possibly create anything more beautiful than what I saw, I have tried only to recreate it in my prints, that those who saw them might see it too—with me.[23]

By pairing the intensity of his vision with the excellence of his technical mastery, Arms sought to express and share his experience of the spiritual essence of the structure.

Of all the buildings in France that Arms depicted, none had a more powerful effect on him than Chartres Cathedral. Arms rendered the structure several times during his career and devoted more plates to it than any other subject. He discovered several different vantage points from which to depict the cathedral, but his rendering of the north portal in *In Memoriam*, 1939 (F.317, pl. 16), ranks as one of the most powerful images of his *oeuvre*.[24] About Chartres' north portal Arms once commented:

To attempt to describe anything so beautiful, so much the most perfect thing of its kind, as the north portal of the Cathedral of Chartres, is useless for me. It represents, to my mind at least, man's supreme spiritual achievement in stone and mortar, the last word in his effort to embody in a building his own aspirations and emotions. It is the most perfect part of the most perfect church in the world.[25]

In Memoriam, like *Aspiration, La Madeleine, Verneuil-sur-Avre*, matches technical brilliance with a masterful feel for design, detail, and mood. The wealth of sculpture in the porch's triple porticoes seems solid and dense. The low vantage point that Arms assumed leads to a sharply oblique perspective that he articulated with attention to precise details as well as contrasting textures, patterns, and the play of light and shade. Although grounded in the physicalities of this world, the image is infused with an almost other-worldly luminosity and a clarity of image that seem to extend beyond mere mortal vision. Arms thus evoked the expression of the divine that he found in Gothic mortar and stone.

Arms explained in numerous essays that he considered artistic vision and technical mastery to be the foundation, the essential underpinnings, of true art. A person who wrote with the same elaborate wording and detail as he approached his printmaking, Arms expressed this attitude quite succinctly in one statement before elaborating more fully:

I like to think of a work of art as having two principal aspects, namely the spiritual and the technical. By the former I mean that which the artist imparts to his expression, in whatever form, which makes of that expression art; by the latter I mean simply the way in which he does it. One is an abstract, intangible thing which we may feel but not necessarily understand, the other is something which is there for all men to see....It is when the two attributes come together, when the great artist and the great technician are one, that we have the great result.[26]

Arms discovered confirmation of what was, for him, a guiding principle in his artmaking, within his subjects, the very fabric of Gothic structures. After commenting that, "I have spoken of the union, in a great etching, of the spiritual conception and the technical power of expressing it," he also explained that "in the Gothic churches of France these same two qualities are perfectly blended.[27]

Although conceptual depth and technical dexterity are both essential to artmaking, Arms did not assign them equal weight. For Arms, the spiritual element was paramount:

> *Between the two there is no comparison in importance. It is the thought which a man has to give the world that makes for him his place in the minds of posterity, not the language....Better the true artist who is a clumsy technician than the most accomplished virtuoso with nothing to say.[28]*

Troubled by self-doubt, Arms feared that his prints were not fully successful. As if about *In Memoriam*, he wrote:

> *When I ask myself if the spiritual (the thought, the spirit, the motivating impulse) has kept pace with the technical in my work, I cannot answer. I know I feel intensely, deeply, and I know I ache to express my feelings on copper. I know, too, that I am in command of a fairly adequate vocabulary. Granted these two, the results should always be what I would have them. But they rarely are. Somewhere between the impulse I experience when I face the Cathedral of Chartres and the proof from the plate I have etched to express that impulse, something, I do not know what, has gone wrong. Either the feeling is not intense enough, or the imagination lacks the power necessary to create a masterpiece, or my hand does not possess the skill to interpret that which is within me. I cannot tell.[29]*

Commentary on Arms' work published during his lifetime and after have suggested concern that Arms was too much a technician recording his subjects as precisely and accurately as possible. One critic wrote in an exhibition review that Arms' works:

> *raise several vital aesthetic issues concerning the artistic value of an art that is mainly interested in technical problems for the sake of reproducing, faithfully, some part of objective reality. Can it have the artistic value of an art whose content is essentially the product of the artist's creative vision and transforming technique?[30]*

Arms himself suspected that technical mastery overshadowed the spiritual component of his prints. He confessed that:

> *It is true that I have always been deeply, absorbingly interested in technical expression....I wanted, and still desperately want, to be a great etcher, though I know now I never shall be. Spiritual conception and power of imagination cannot be acquired, technique can.[31]*

An exchange of unusually honest and soul-searching letters between Arms and Carl Zigrosser, a dealer turned curator who worked tirelessly in the promotion of American printmaking, drew from Arms in 1941 one of his most thoughtful comments on the expressive nature of his prints:

I have always believed myself to be, fundamentally, a mystic, in spite of the hard, bright literalness of my work. It got hard and bright not because I felt the Gothic Spirit could best be expressed by literal representation, in hard, bright, imitative terms, but because, steeped in mystical wonder at, and devotion to, Gothic art and the spirit that produced it, <u>my</u> interpretation of that spirit came out in those particular terms. A contradiction, you will say, for mysticism cannot be expressed in literalness. But there you have it, that is what has happened in my case.[32]

It is true that in some plates, especially panoramic views of cities and towns such as in *Venetian Mirror*, 1935 (F.289) and *Reflections at Finchingfield, England*, 1938 (F.311, fig. 38), the extraordinary weight of dispassionately precise detail and even contrast of light and shade may detract from an overall sense of compositional harmony. Although *Reflections at Finchingfield, England* is a technical tour de force, Arms' uniformity of treatment, his delineation of reflections across a broad expanse of water with detail almost equal to that which they mirror, deny a sense of focus and compositional rhythm in the print. Impressive in its visual literalness, it nonetheless seems to lack pictorial and emotional excitement.

Arms' technical accomplishments, however, did successfully merge with his profound awareness of Gothic spirituality in prints from his various series. His facility with etching provided the vehicle for the creation of some of the most memorable prints of his career, including *In Memoriam* and *Aspiration, La Madeleine, Verneuil-sur-Avre* as well as *Stanwick Churchyard*, 1939 (F.324), *Puerta del Obispo, Zamora* (fig. 33), and *Study in Stone, Cathedral of Orense*, 1933 (F.257, fig. 39). With *In Memoriam* and *Aspiration, La Madeleine, Verneuil-sur-Avre*, Arms only examined the structures, stripping away extraneous motifs representing the everyday life of the secular world—figures, houses, activities, etc.—and effaced stylistic elements suggestive of the hand or mind of the artist, such as personal and spontaneous linework. Arms removed the subjects from the here-and-now of the real world and introduced an almost hallucinatory clarity to the scenes with the very crispness, literalness, and precision with which he delineated the buildings and the exactitude with which he captured the contrast of light and shade.

Figure 38
Reflections at Finchingfield, England, 1938
Etching
7⅛ x 17³⁄₁₆ in.
(18.1 x 43.7 cm)
Gift of Walter Crandall, 1970
(16,195)

He allowed an eerie silence and quietude to envelop both scenes, as if they exist in an hermetically sealed environment. Mysterious shadows creeping across the pavement and even the foot of La Madeleine contribute further to the dreamlike quality of the images. The images are so quiet, so precise, so removed from this life that they assume divine proportions, as if Arms represented a higher level of existence. Like the transparent eyeball of the nineteenth-century American transcendentalists, Arms subsumed himself within his subjects, and a sense of mystical spirituality resulted.

During the 1920s, 30s, and 40s, Arms also etched general views of many of the cities and towns that he and his wife Dorothy visited during their tours of Spain, France, Italy, and England. *Burgos*, 1924 (F.142, fig. 40), a striking view of the

Figure 40
Burgos, 1924
Etching
8⅝ x 13¹/₁₆ in.
(21.9 x 33.2 cm)
Gift of Richard H.
and Helen T.
Hagemeyer, 1988
(20,485)

cathedral's towers and spires soaring over a hill that obscures its foundations, is an early such work from Spain; *"This England" (Fairford, Gloucestershire)*, 1952 (F.426), an evocative view of the town of Fairford in Gloucestershire, followed almost 30 years later and was one of the last prints of Arms' career. *Le Puy*, 1928 (F.214, fig. 41) typifies the distant perspective that Arms adopted for many such views. The city is set among a series of volcanic cones, two of which are surmounted by religious monuments, including an enormous sculpture of the Virgin Mary and a small 10th-century oratory.

The city of Venice captured Arms' imagination in a way no other city did. Although not filled with Gothic churches and cathedrals, the city is a monument to medieval architecture, as its palazzi and grand civic buildings, dating from as early as the 14th century, attest. The aging city of crumbling stone, shimmering water, and vaporous light inspired an especially lovely set of images by Arms, a group that reveals Arms' compositional skills at their best. During 1930 and 1931, the artist devoted eight major plates to Venetian subjects, and then one more in 1935, leading to probably the most cohesive group of prints of his long career. The Academy is fortunate to possess fine impressions of six of the eight works.

Shadows of Venice, 1930 (F.229, pl. 17) depicts the Ponte di Rialto, a sixteenth-century bridge lined with shops over the Grand Canal. Arms created a striking composition of repeating architectural motifs ranging from steps, balustrades, and balconies to the arches of an arcade and the bold conceit of one arch framing another. The blue toned paper on which the Academy's impression is printed lends a silvery delicacy to the composition's patterns of light and shade, murky reflective water, and weathered stone. *Shadows of Venice* silently evokes qualities generally associated with the floating city— diffused color, soft light, and watery atmosphere.

The Enchanted Doorway, Venezia, 1930 (F.227, fig. 42) is the second print in the series and presents a 15th-century archway adjacent to the Basilica of San Marcos on the Piazza San Marco. The composition is forthright in its frontality and stable gridlike design, but all sense of mass and weight dissipates in Venice's decorative patterns of brick, stone, and sculpture.

La Bella Venezia, 1930 (F.232, fig. 43), stands in dramatic opposition to *The Enchanted Doorway*. Instead of the visual excitement of nonstop patterning and geometric games, *La Bella Venezia* presents from across the San Marco Canal a subdued yet unerringly detailed panorama of Venice around the Piazza San Marco. A careful examination of the print reveals not only the towering Campanile, but to its right the two stone columns dedicated to St. Mark and St. Theodore, the gateway and enormous clock of the Torre dell'Orologio, the intricately arcaded Doges' Palace, and the domes of the Basilica of San Marco beyond. Arms recognized the abstract potential of buildings along the shoreline and turned the sequence of structures into a horizontal pattern activated by the variations in roofline and facade treatment. Western convention would have led Arms to situate this horizontal band low in the picture plane and allow the sky to fill the remainder of the composition. Arms ignored convention and, as in Japanese *ukiyo-e* prints, tipped the scene's perspective, flattened the sense of space, and daringly placed the line of buildings across the upper third of the plate. As the line of buildings crosses the side edges of the plate, it locks itself into position, allowing the top of the Campanile to approach the top margin with tantalizing closeness. Unlike *Venetian Mirror* and *Reflections at Finchingfield, England*, in which the precise

Figure 41
Le Puy, 1928
Etching
9¾ x 13¹/₁₆ in.
(24.8 x 33.2 cm)
Gift of Richard H.
and Helen T.
Hagemeyer, 1991
(21,163)

delineation of reflections is an important component in the careful depiction of the sites, Arms allowed the mirroring effect of summarily suggested faint reflections to reiterate the abstract horizontal patterning of the buildings. He also played the flat expanse of toned and relatively unmarked paper against the visual weight of the buildings. In this image of elegant understatement, Arms cleverly manipulated space, design, and perception.

Venetian Filigree, 1931 (F.235, fig. 44) represents a continuation of Arms' experimentation with design, abstraction, and perception. The print depicts the Ca' d'Oro, one of the most frequently depicted and photographed palazzi in Venice.[33] The "Golden House" is famous for the intricate and delicate tracery which, now bare of ornamentation, was originally gilded. Arms expressed the richness of the facade with masterful precision, creating an extraordinary breadth of tone through linework alone. In this luminous image of shuttered doors, darkened balconies, and silent reflection, Arms emphasized the palazzo's rich repetition of pattern and cursive design. He pressed the facade against the picture plane and allowed it to fill the plate to the exclusion of its surrounding context. In this way, Arms all but eliminated from the print the third dimension and emphasized the flat abstract patterning of the facade. The reflections in the water connect seamlessly with the design of the facade, reinforcing the abstract two-dimensionality of the print. The design is so bold, so flat, and so abstract that the image starts to become disturbingly disorienting. Which way is up? What is real and what is reflection? What is real and what is illusion? The composition calls into question the fundamental premises of the image and the viewer's perception of it.

From 1920, the year in which Arms published the first print in the *Gargoyle Series*, to 1952, when he completed the last works in the *English Series* and *French Church Series*, Arms created 126 major plates celebrating the heart and soul of Gothic architecture. Throughout his life, he responded with reverence and awe to the physical beauty of the structures, their "grandeur of scale, beauty of proportion and abundant wealth of detail."[34] He also was moved by the power of their mystical essence. To Arms, Gothic architecture represented "the most spiritual and significant expression of his aspirations

Figure 42
The Enchanted Doorway, Venezia, 1930
Etching
12⅝ x 6⅝ in.
(32.1 x 16.8 cm)
Gift of Richard H. and Helen T. Hagemeyer, 1990
(20,850)

that man has yet created in terms of stone and glass and metal."[35] His deeply felt identification with the truth, beauty, and spirituality of medieval times led Arms to create a large body of work characterized by extraordinary technical merit, sincerity of effort, and emotional depth. In an autobiographical statement composed in 1930, at a time when his printmaking was first reaching its greatest power, Arms paid tribute to the source of his creativity and summarized his printmaking hopes. Although he wrote only in terms of his work in France, the meaning of his words hold true for his other European architectural subjects:

> *I have followed [Gothic structures] from one end of France to the other; I have worked in the shadow of their magnificent portals and climbing apses; and always they have given me fresh inspiration and renewed resolution to interpret, in so far as my limited power will permit, the imagery of their beauty.*[36]

As a printmaker, Arms worked for his own personal satisfaction and as an act of reverence, a means of expressing his faith in the divine. Arms also felt what he considered a larger purpose, an obligation to his fellow human beings. He wished to share with them the joy, the sense of peace and continuity, the spiritual refreshment that he experienced on the contemplation of his subjects. In an essay titled "Credo," Arms commented that works of art are:

> *not mere representations, or even interpretations, of places, people, and things, but, in the last analysis, the innermost thoughts, the most poignant feelings, of their creators, expressed in terms of line and tone and color....[My works] are the concrete expression of my emotional and intellectual being, of heart and mind, and of the creative force which transforms the concept into tangible form. Each is a message from me to you, the effort not only to tell you of the architectural beauty of some great church...or the natural loveliness of a bit of countryside, but, more important to me at least, the feelings I have experienced in the contemplation of these things. They will possess meaning, interest, and merit, in your eyes just to the degree to which I have been able to convey, and you to receive, this message.*[37]

Figure 43
La Bella Venezia,
1930
Etching printed
in brown ink
7¼ x 16½ in.
(18.4 x 41.9 cm)
Gift of Richard H.
and Helen T.
Hagemeyer, 1990
(20,853)

1. Arms, "John Taylor Arms," [pp. 4–5].
2. John Taylor Arms, *Gothic Memories, Etchings and Drawings* (New York: Wm. C. Popper & Co., [1938]), [p. 3].
3. *Ibid.*, [p. 4].
4. *Ibid.*, [p. 6].
5. *Ibid.*, [p. 5].
6. Catherine Hoover Voorsanger, "Dictionary of Architects, Artisans, Artists, and Manufacturers," in *In Pursuit of Beauty: Americans and the Aesthetic Movement*, exh. cat. (New York: The Metropolitan Museum of Art and Rizzoli International Publications, Inc., 1986), p. 423.
7. See New York, The Metropolitan Museum of Art, *In Pursuit of Beauty, Americans and the Aesthetic Movement*.
8. Bassham, *John Taylor Arms*, pp. 5–6.
9. Arms etched the thirteenth plate in the *Gargoyle Series* in 1929 and the fourteenth in 1947.
10. Arms, "John Taylor Arms," [p. 4].
11. As an ironic twist to the history of Notre Dame and Arms' depiction of it, it is interesting to note that its gargoyles were a nineteenth century addition by Eugène Emmanuel Viollet-le-Duc. A French architect, engineer, and archaeologist, Viollet-le-Duc led the restoration of numerous Gothic structures, including the Cluniac abbey at Vézelay and Paris' Notre Dame. As an architect himself and fully steeped in the history of Western styles, Arms was no doubt familiar with the work of this proponent of medieval architecture. Perhaps Arms approached his representation of Le Stryge with a smile, recognizing a nineteenth-century act of Gothic Revivalism much in sympathy with his own interests.
12. For a detailed discussion of Arms' *Gargoyle Series* and gargoyle imagery by Cameron, Meryon, and Pennell see S. William Pelletier, "The Gargoyle Images of John Taylor Arms," *Print Quarterly* 7, no. 3 (Sept. 1990), pp. 292–303.

Figure 44
Venetian Filigree,
1931
Etching
10¾ x 11 in.
(27.3 x 27.9 cm)
Gift of James Jensen
and Jennifer Saville
in honor of Richard
H. and Helen T.
Hagemeyer, 1993
(24,081)

13. Bassham, *John Taylor Arms*, p. 7. In addition to introducing dots to create tonal effects, Arms also began to rely on patterns of repeating dotted lines to lend inflection to areas of texture, pattern, and tone.

14. Arms, *Exhibition of Drawings, Including Work in Yucatan and Mexico*, [pp. 2–3].

15. Dorothy Noyes Arms and John Taylor Arms, *Churches of France* (New York: The Macmillan Company, 1929); Dorothy Noyes Arms and John Taylor Arms, *Hill Towns and Cities of Northern Italy* (New York: The Macmillan Company, 1932).

16. Arms described how he created an etching in a series of three articles published in late 1940 and early 1941: "John Taylor Arms Tells How He Makes an Etching, Part 1—Preparation of Plate," *American Artist* 4, no. 12 (Dec. 1940), pp. 14–16; "John Taylor Arms Tells How He Makes an Etching, Part 2—Drawing On and Etching the Plate," *American Artist* 5, no. 1 (Jan. 1941), pp. 10–12; "John Taylor Arms Tells How He Makes an Etching, Part 3—Printing," *American Artist* 5, no. 2 (Feb. 1941), pp. 13–15.

17. Journal of John Taylor Arms, dated Seville, Sept. 10, [year not recorded] (John Taylor Arms Papers, 65:19–20, AAA).

18. *Ibid.*, dated Seville, Sept. 11, 65:20.

19. *Ibid.*, dated Seville, Sept. 12, 65:21.

20. *Ibid.*, dated Palencia, Oct. 27, 1932, 65:385.

21. Arms and Arms, *Churches of France*, pp. 50–51.

22. Arms, "John Taylor Arms," [p. 4].

23. Arms, "Self Estimate," p. 10.

24. The title of the work reflects Arms' dedication of the print to his mother-in-law on its publication in 1939 after her death the preceding year.

25. Warren Wheelock, "John Taylor Arms: Modern Mediaevalist," *Art Instruction* 3, no. 2 (Feb. 1939), p. 18.

26. Arms, "John Taylor Arms," [p. 2]. See also Arms, "Self Estimate," p. 7; John Taylor Arms, "Credo," in *Selected Examples from Thirty Years of Etching, John Taylor Arms*, exh. cat. (New York: Kennedy & Company, 1945), pp. 7–8.

27. Arms, "John Taylor Arms," [p. 5].

28. *Ibid.*, [p. 2].

29. Arms, "Self Estimate," p. 9.

30. "New Exhibitions of the Week, J.T. Arms: Twenty-One Years of Drawing," p. 16. See also Watrous, *A Century of American Printmaking*, pp. 80–81.

31. Arms, "Self Estimate," pp. 8–9.

32. Letter from John Taylor Arms to Carl Zigrosser, dated Fairfield, CT, Sept. 12, 1941 (Carl Zigrosser Papers, 4613:743, AAA).

33. For instance, Ernest Roth etched *Ca' d'Oro* in 1913 and Donald Shaw MacLaughlan created his version, also known as *Ca' d'Oro*, in 1922. Even Arthur Wesley Dow diagramed the facade of the palazzo in his discussion of rectangular designs in his art instruction book. See Arthur Wesley Dow, *Composition*, p. 41.

34. Arms, "John Taylor Arms," [p. 4].

35. Arms, "Self Estimate," p. 10.

36. Arms, "John Taylor Arms," [p. 5].

37. Arms, "Credo," pp. 6–7.

From the Miniature to the Monumental:
Arms' Other Prints

At the same time that Arms was preoccupied with the development of his major New York and European architectural plates, he also devoted time, thought, and energy to a variety of other series and subjects. Over the course of his career, Arms initiated work in nine additional series, several of which will be discussed in this chapter and next. Three series, the *Demonstration Series*, *Miniature Series*, and *Christmas Card Series*, are represented by numerous plates etched over the course of several years; another series, the *Yucatán Series*, reaches to just one work published in 1940. Arms also etched several works which stand by themselves, unrelated to a designated series. However, with few exceptions, such as one still-life subject and large-scale landscape (pls. 5, 20), architectural subjects remain a constant throughout all of these prints just as they are with the majority of the work examined heretofore.

Like Adolph Dehn, Thomas Handforth, Troy Kinney, and other American print-makers working during the first half of this century, Arms often devoted one small plate per year to extending seasonal greetings to friends, relatives, and associates. Initiating the tradition in 1916 shortly after learning how to etch, Arms periodically created Christmas cards through 1944, ultimately concluding the *Christmas Card Series* with a total of seventeen published plates.

Merry Xmas from Dorothy and John Arms, 1920, 1920 (F.57, pl. 18), is one of his most charming Christmas-card designs, with two song birds perched on a roughly constructed wood sign inscribed, "To Happiness—1921." An early work etched with aquatint, it relates to Arms' other plates of 1919 and 1920 created with the same medium. The association between this Christmas card and works such as *Moonlight, Number One* (pl. 8) and *The Butterfly* (fig. 20) extends beyond Arms' dependence on the same medium in the three prints. This Christmas card represents an elaboration of Arms' considerations of Japanese woodblock prints or of their principles as filtered through the teachings and prints of Arthur Wesley Dow, as already addressed in both instances. Appealing close-up images of birds, tree branches, and the moon enjoy a long tradition within the *oeuvre* of Japanese *ukiyo-e* and *shin hanga* printmakers such as Hiroshige Utagawa and Sôzan Itô. Watanabe Shôzaburô, a major publisher and exporter of *shin hanga* prints, commissioned bird-and-flower works and exported them to the West as early as 1908.[1] The tonal qualities, flattened space, and truncation of forms of *Merry Xmas from Dorothy and John Arms* are strongly reminiscent of the work of the Japanese masters as they are of diagrams published by Dow in *Composition*.[2]

Arms selected a variety of subjects for the Christmas cards, ranging from the bird design of *Merry Xmas from Dorothy and John Arms* to the homey depiction of his housefront and doorway in *Our Studio Door*, 1922 (F.125, fig. 45), several European

Figure 45
Our Studio Door,
1922
Etching
5⅛ x 3¾ in.
(13.0 x 9.5 cm)
Purchase, C.
Montague Cooke,
Jr. Fund, 1993
(24,080)

architectural subjects and city views, and, in the last plate of the series, a remarkable miniature landscape view of the Vermont hills in *Vermont,* 1944 (F.384, fig. 46), as seen from Arms' summer studio.[3]

Many of Arms' plates serve double duty, appearing in more than one set of prints. Multiple assignments occur for several of the works in the *Christmas Card Series* and the *Miniature Series.* Prints in both groups are also part of the European architectural suites discussed in the preceding chapter. Illustrating another crossover, the Christmas card *Vermont* is also an outstanding image in the *Miniature Series.*

Miniature prints enjoyed general popularity as a compositional format and challenge among American printmakers and collectors around the middle of this century. The newly organized Miniature Print Society issued its first print in 1941, distributing impressions to its subscribing members.[4] At that time, Arms wrote about the founding of the society and discussed the criteria that defines a miniature. He commented that although the society stipulated that its miniature prints were to measure "not more than five inches in any dimension…it is to be hoped that, in order that they may be true 'miniatures,' it will be kept less than this."[5] Arms clarified the concept of "miniature prints" by indicating that small size alone does not a miniature make. He commented that the designation "miniature" relates to "the technique the artist employed in making [the print], a technique which must be at a scale commensurate with the dimensions of the plate."[6] In other words, concept and design are as important as dimensions to the creation of a miniature.

Arms was keenly interested in miniatures as a printmaker as well as a print connoisseur. The small scale of miniature prints must have been an enjoyable challenge for Arms, given his remarkable technical dexterity and interest in design. In approaching his miniature prints, Arms took his own words to heart, filling his plates with satisfyingly

Figure 46
Vermont, 1944
Etching
1⁵⁄₁₆ x 2⅜ in.
(3.3 x 6.0 cm)
Gift of Walter
Crandall, 1953
(13,231)

complete and cohesive compositions devoted to various themes related to the rest of his *oeuvre.*[7] The *Miniature Series* includes images of gargoyles; corbels, figures, and other sculptural details; Gothic churches and cathedrals and additional architectural monuments; street scenes; and landscapes among other subjects.

New York from Staten Island Ferry of 1917 (fig. 16), already discussed as one of Arms' earliest prints and one of his two drypoints, was the inaugural print in his *Miniature Series*. "Black and White," *Trébrivan* (F.423) dating from 1953, the year of Arms' death, concludes the series as its forty-first and final plate. Measuring only 1⁵⁄₁₆ by 2⅜ inches, *Vermont* is an exquisite print presenting the state's lush countryside. With a close look, it is possible to discern a patchwork-pattern of fields across rolling hills which are further articulated by trees, a curving road, and reflective body of water. The rendering of such detail with such precision seems inconceivable until one understands Arms' working technique. Arms possessed a fine collection of etching needles, but kept them stored safely away for personal enjoyment beyond actual use: "Etching needles exert an irresistible fascination on me and I always buy one when I see a new kind. These I keep neatly arranged in a little chest of drawers beside my work bench, a source of infinite pride."[8] Instead, Arms relied on something a little bit more mundane for his etching, "an ordinary sewing needle (ranging in size from 5 to 10) set in a wooden handle with a metal cap, which just suits my hand."[9] The fine points of his sewing needles used in tandem with magnifying glasses, sometimes as many as three in a series, allowed Arms to draw with microscopically fine lines and dots.[10]

Stokesay Castle, 1942 (F.369, pl. 19), the thirtieth print in the *Miniature Series* and ninth in the *English Series*, also typifies Arms' ability to match his subject to the miniature format.[11] The tower, buttresses, and other parts of the aging castle constitute a pleasing design of architectural forms, rhythms, and contrast enlivened by a diagonal axis of spatial recession. The design also fits proportionally onto the small-scale plate of 2⁵⁄₁₆ x 3¹⁄₁₆ inches.

When Arms etched this work during the early years of World War II, the plate assumed particular personal significance. Since travel to Europe was impossible during the war years, Arms based the print on a sketch rendered on an earlier visit. The creation of this plate was for Arms an act of reflection on peace and beauty:

> *I turned for relief and respite to a remote bit of England of pre-war days....Buried in its quiet English countryside, itself a relic of another day, Stokesay Castle is to me a symbol of a beauty known and loved long ago, of something that is gone out of a life beset with the problems and struggles of a bitter present, but something whose memory will not pass because it is part of that beauty we all crave and cling to in times of doubt and fear and trouble.*[12]

Although travel restrictions during World War II curtailed Arms' trips to Europe, he and his family nonetheless discovered adventure elsewhere. February 1940 found them in Mexico where Arms spent time sketching in Taxco and on the Yucatán Peninsula. Arms commenced work on what turned into two short-lived series of prints, the *Mexican Series* and the *Yucatán Series*. The former is comprised of two works, *Shadows in Mexico (Sketch)*, 1940 (F.340A, fig. 50) and *Light and Shade, Taxco*, 1946 (F.394, fig. 47); the *Yucatán Series* is based on a single image, *Plumed Serpent, Chichén Itzá*, 1940 (F.344, fig. 48).

Arms' journal entries record his pleasure in these new subjects. When he arrived in Chichén Itzá, one the most famous sacred temple and pyramid complexes in Mexico, he "didn't stop to unpack but rushed right off to ruins." He then related his response to

the site and his activities: "Very impressive. Climbed up on top of pyramid & started sketch of detail of Temple of the Warriors."[13] This sketch did not lead to a print, but a drawing created over the following three days provided the basis of *Plumed Serpent, Chichén Itzá*. About the source of that work, Arms first noted briefly, "Finished my drawing [of Temple of the Warriors] and started one of great heads of serpents.... Chichén is good for detail but poor for mass." Two days later he remarked, "Finished my small drawing of serpent's head....This is truly a most wonderful place."[14]

Plumed Serpent, Chichén Itzá is not only part of the *Miniature Series,* it is also the sole print in the *Yucatán Series.* Arms carefully described the serpent with detail and a range of tone that passes from the deep shadow enveloping its eye through the delicate half-shadows illuminating the interior of its mouth, to the highlights that pick out each feather, each decorative motif, each pit in the living stone. Just as Arms' gargoyles preside over their domains with intriguing animation, this plumed serpent represents part of the in"animate" fabric of the monument. Nonetheless, as a curiously appealing figural detail, it addresses the viewer with a benign friendliness. Through this sculptural motif, Arms again recognized and celebrated the enduring spirituality of historic architectural monuments.

Arms was at work in Taxco, an old mining town high in the Sierra Madre Mountains, by the end of February.[15] The Spanish founded Taxco in the early sixteenth century, and it became one of the key colonial crossroads and trade-route stops. The Spanish baroque church of Santa Prisca, dating from 1759, presides over the town as it spills down the slope. Arms remarked in his journal: "Taxco is one of the most picturesque towns I have ever seen. Grand views, remarkable...cathedral, mountain scenery." Then he started to sketch it: "At work on drawing of whole

town (from hotel entrance) at 6:45....
Drew the cathedral & blocked out the
town."[16] Arms published the sweeping
panoramic view of the town in 1946 as
the finely toned and detailed *Light and
Shade, Taxco* (fig. 47).

Arms often exhibited new work with
his New York dealer Kennedy & Company,
and his prints were regularly seen in exhibitions across the country. Arms received
numerous awards for his prints throughout his career, with *Light and Shade, Taxco*

Figure 48
*Plumed Serpent,
Chichén Itzá*, 1940
Etching
1¹⁵⁄₁₆ x 2½ in.
(4.9 x 6.4 cm)
Gift of James F.
Jensen in memory
of Joseph Feher,
1987 (19,800)

receiving more than any other image. In four years it garnered ten citations, including
the First Prize for Graphic Art in the 124th annual exhibition of New York's National
Academy of Design, one of the premier exhibitions of the American art establishment.[17]

Throughout his life Arms was an avid outdoorsman, with a passion for fishing. His
interest in the back woods led first to summers spent in Maine and the creation of a
summer studio in North Pomfret, Vermont, to which he and his wife retreated each
year for time spent etching, writing, and fishing. No doubt it was this same interest that
led Arms, while vacationing in Wyoming in the summer of 1932, to draw and etch the
Valley of the Savery. Dorothy Arms described the beauty and remoteness of the valley as
well as the difficulty they experienced in getting there by car and foot.[18] For two days
Arms perched on the edge of the valley and sketched the sweeping panoramic view he
termed "wonderful, stark, [and] monumental."[19] Arms later etched the vista in *The
Valley of the Savery, Wyoming*, 1934 (F.276, pl. 20).

The comparison of an impression of *The Valley of the Savery* with its preliminary
drawing (fig. 49), both in the Academy's collection, provide interesting perspectives on
Arms' work. Arms sketched the view with a very fine pencil point on the smooth surface
of fragile tissue. With silvery contour lines, he described the basic view and suggested
the sweeping slope of the foreground; with parallel strokes of shading, he suggested the
planar escarpments coursing through the valley; and with delicate patchwork-patterned
hatching, he blocked in the basic massing of trees. A girder bridge and narrow road
humanize the scene. The drawing is an elegant composition of rhythmic swelling
curves, opposing patterns, and balance of light and shade, mass and unmarked paper.

The etching relates very closely to the drawing, the most obvious difference
between the two being the reversal of the printed image. Arms was not overly
concerned with systematically reversing his images before drawing them on his
ground-covered plates; he did not believe that orientation pertained to the aesthetic
value of the work. For Arms, only well-known subjects, such as familiar architectural and city views, warranted the extra step of reversing a drawing prior to working on
the plate.[20] Arms retained in the etching of *The Valley of the Savery* the overall delicacy
of the drawing, its generalization of form and sense of panoramic breadth, but
strengthened the contrast of light and shade throughout the composition. As Arms
downplayed the detailed hatching of the trees and generalized their massing, he directed
more attention to the articulation of the valley escarpments. Various patterns of shading
and hatching lend an architectural quality to the simple, prismatic definition of the sheer
rock faces, but do not smother the work's harmony of articulated shape, deep space,
and sweeping vista.

Plate 12
The Sarah Jane,
New York, 1920
Etching, aquatint
$10^{3}/_{8}$ x $7^{3}/_{8}$ in.
(26.4 x 18.7 cm)
Gift of Eliza Lefferts
and Charles
Montague Cooke,
Jr., 1927 (6520)

Plate 13
The Gates of the City,
1922
Etching, aquatint
printed in color
8⅞ x 8½ in.
(22.5 x 21.6 cm)
Purchase, C.
Montague Cooke, Jr.
Fund, 1987 (19,947)

Plate 14
An American Cathedral, 1921
Etching printed
in brown ink
17¼ x 6¹³⁄₁₆ in.
(43.8 x 17.3 cm)
Gift of Richard H.
and Helen T.
Hagemeyer, 1989
(20,634)

Plate 15
Rodez, 1927
Etching
11⅞ x 4¹⁵⁄₁₆ in.
(30.2 x 12.5 cm)
Gift of Richard H.
and Helen T.
Hagemeyer, 1990
(20,835)

John Taylor Arms

Plate 16
In Memoriam, 1939
Etching
14⅝ x 12 in.
(37.2 x 30.5 cm)
Purchase, 1941
(11,811)

Plate 17
Shadows of Venice,
1930
Etching, aquatint on
blue-gray paper
10¼ x 12⅛ in.
(26.0 x 30.8 cm)
Gift of Richard H.
and Helen T.
Hagemeyer, 1990
(20,851)

John Taylor Arms

Plate 18
Merry Xmas from Dorothy and John Arms, 1920, 1920
Etching, aquatint printed in green ink
5½ x 4¼ in.
(14.0 x 10.8 cm)
Gift of Richard H. and Helen T. Hagemeyer, 1993
(24,032)

Plate 19
Stokesay Castle, 1942
Etching on green paper
2⁵⁄₁₆ x 3¹⁄₁₆ in.
(5.9 x 7.8 cm)
Gift of Eliza Lefferts and Charles Montague Cooke, Jr., 1943
(11,990)

Plate 20
*The Valley of the
Savery, Wyoming*,
1934
Etching printed on
green-gray paper
$7^{13}/_{16}$ x $14^{3}/_{16}$ in.
(19.8 x 36.0 cm)
Gift of Richard H.
and Helen T.
Hagemeyer, 1990
(20,864)

Carl Zigrosser, the print dealer, curator, and critic whose opinion Arms valued perhaps more than any other person in the art world, paid Arms the compliment of publicly praising *The Valley of the Savery* at New York's Grolier Club. Arms responded in letter form, articulating his formal approach to the subject and attributing the success of the work to Zigrosser's influence. He said that he:

> stressed [in the print] those qualities which you helped teach me are essential to a work of art—emphasis on design, simplification, elimination of extraneous detail, concentration on the expression of an idea, the triumph of the spiritual element over the means taken to achieve it.[21]

A comparison of *The Valley of the Savery* with Arms' earlier efforts in the *Maine Series*, Arms' only other attempts in landscape, seems appropriate. *Beaver House* (fig. 13) and *"Pete" and "Topsy"* (fig. 12), works previously alluded to in association with the *Maine Series*, reflect Arms' early awareness of the nineteenth-century's etching revival. The earlier work bears the intimacy in scale and subject that characterizes the prints of artist-etchers such as Charles François Daubigny and which Arms rejected in *The Valley of the Savery*. Instead a grandeur of conception and breadth of vision provide the foundation for the later print. Just as Arms distanced his architectural printmaking from the scribbly or "personalized" linework learned from artists such as Seymour Haden, so too did he efface himself from the creation of this scene. Precision in draftsmanship, clarity of image, and brilliance of tonal contrast, familiar qualities in Arms' mature prints, are at its heart. Indeed, *The Valley of the Savery*, especially in the definition of the escarpments, shares with Arms' other mature prints a sense of structural solidity. As Arms was said to have remarked, he discovered "the architectural quality of the landscape."[22]

As unusual as this print might appear in Arms' *oeuvre* because of its scale as a landscape image, it is closely linked to his other works conceptually and stylistically. Although

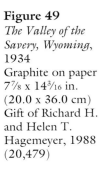

Figure 49
The Valley of the Savery, Wyoming, 1934
Graphite on paper
7⅞ x 14³/₁₆ in.
(20.0 x 36.0 cm)
Gift of Richard H. and Helen T. Hagemeyer, 1988
(20,479)

Arms did not address architectural subjects to the exclusion of all else in his *oeuvre*, they were an abiding interest throughout a career that pushed forty years. He felt his mission was to share with others the inspiration of truth and beauty, as he experienced it himself. He also worked to promote printmaking in a practical way, through a second career as spokesman, writer, and educator.

1. Okamoto Hiromi and Henry D. Smith II, "Ukiyo-e for Modern Japan: The Legacy of Watanabe Shòzaburò," in *The New Wave, Twentieth-Century Japanese Prints from the Robert O. Muller Collection*, p. 29.

2. Dow, *Composition*, pp. 25, 35, 62–64, 83–85.

3. Letter from John Taylor Arms to Thornton Oakley, dated Fairfield, CT, Feb. 4, 1945 (Thornton Oakley Papers, 4394:1220, AAA).

4. James Swann's drypoint of 1941, *Winter in Texas*, was the first publication of the Miniature Print Society; the edition numbered 200 prints. See Honolulu Academy of Arts' records for its impression of the work (HAA 11,800).

5. John Taylor Arms, "Printmaking Notes and Activities, Miniature Prints," *Print* 2, no. 2 (Summer 1941), p. 77.

6. *Ibid.*, p. 77.

7. Despite Arms' published position on dimensions, however, five of his designated miniatures exceed the five inch limit! This figure is based on dimensions published in Fletcher's catalogue raisonné. See *Chapiteau Gothique, Dorothy et John Taylor Arms, A.D. MCMXXVI*, 1926 (F.185); *A Saint, Chartres*, 1927 (F.199); *A Breton Calvary*, 1932 (F.247); *Anglia Antiqua, West Walton*, 1937 (F.310); and *Stranger in England, St. Lawrence, West Wycombe, Buckinghamshire*, 1940 (F.336).

8. Pelletier, "*John Taylor Arms: An American Mediaevalist*," p. 930.

9. *Ibid.*, p. 930.

10. *Ibid.*, p. 930.

11. Arms participated with the Miniature Print Society in the publication and distribution to its membership of miniature prints. The society published and distributed *Stokesay Castle* in 1943. See accession records for the Academy's impression of the print (HAA 11,990).

12. John Taylor Arms, "Stokesay Castle," *News of Fine Prints*, no. 2 (April 1943), p. 1, John Taylor Arms vertical file, Prints Division, New York Public Library, New York.

13. Journal of John Taylor Arms, dated Chichén Itzá, Feb. 8, 1940 (John Taylor Arms Papers, 65:443, AAA).

14. *Ibid.*, dated Chichén Itzá, Feb. 9, 1940, (65:443) and Feb. 11, 1940 (65:444).

15. *Ibid.*, dated Taxco, Feb. 27, 1940, (65:452).

16. *Ibid.*, dated Taxco, Feb. 27 and 28, 1940, (65:452, 453).

17. See Pelletier, "John Taylor Arms, His World and Work," pp. 103–108 for a complete listing of Arms' print awards.

18. Dorothy Noyes Arms, "Romance in the Making of Prints" in *The Romance of Fine Prints*, edited by Alfred Fowler (Kansas City: The Print Society, 1938), pp. 39–40.

19. Letter from John Taylor Arms to Carl Zigrosser, dated Fairfield, CT, Mar. 13, 1946 (Carl Zigrosser Papers, 4613:769, AAA); see also journal of John Taylor Arms, dated Aug. 24 and 25, 1932 (John Taylor Arms Papers, 65:352–353, AAA).

20. Arms, "John Taylor Arms Tells How He Makes an Etching, Part 2," p. 10. The examination of his *oeuvre* partially bears out this professed tenet—scenes of well-known sites such as Venice's Ca' d'Oro (*Venetian Filigree*, 1931, F.235, fig. 44) appear accurately; lesser-known structures such as those in Évreux (*Memento Vivere, Notre Dame, Évreux*, 1947, F.407), Louviers (*Louviers Lace*, 1936, F.303), and Verneuil-sur-Avre (*Aspiration, La Madeleine, Verneuil-sur-Avre*, 1939, F.329, fig. 37), appear in reverse. Arms' general views of Chartres, one of the best-known Gothic cathedrals in Europe (*Chartres*, 1927, F.193; *Chartres in Miniature*, 1939, F. 330; and *Chartres, The Magnificent*, 1948, F.411), present the cathedral correctly and incorrectly.

21. Letter from Arms to Carl Zigrosser, dated Fairfield, CT, March 13, 1946 (Carl Zigrosser Papers, 4613:769, AAA).

22. Arms and Arms, "Descriptive Catalogue," plate 280.

Beyond Printmaking:
Arms as Spokesman, Writer, and Educator

A second career devoted to the advocacy for the graphic arts was as important to Arms as the etching of his own plates and the expression of his own artistic vision. When not engaged with his own printmaking pursuits, Arms was involved with the promotion of the graphic arts on a number of different fronts. As curator, educator, author, board member, and consultant, Arms was instrumental in providing organizational support for artists and raising the profile of the graphic arts nationally and internationally on the public and governmental levels. With unflagging energy, he published articles and books, organized print exhibitions, coordinated the affairs of professional societies, educated the public through demonstrations and lectures, and advised agencies about art and printmaking affairs within the United States government. A traditionalist, Arms saw the gulf between his work and beliefs and that of other artists becoming increasingly wide as the decades passed. But he always stood firm in his support of freedom of expression and the need for tolerance of all viewpoints, including those more "modern" than his own.

Arms' efforts to increase public awareness of the graphic arts led to more than 150 public demonstrations of the etching process; in just 1941 he conducted sixteen such programs.[1] Often working on a portable press which he carried with him, Arms demonstrated etching to school, library, museum, art club, community, and business audiences, even before TV cameras, at the New York World's Fair in 1939, and before a crowd gathered outside a Manhattan department store window behind which he was at work.[2] Arms was an eager instructor, willing to put on his show in the New York City metropolitan area, New England, and as far afield as Kansas City, Missouri, and Toronto.[3] One day, Arms took a private plane to an upstate New York factory town, put on a demonstration, and flew home a few hours later.[4] The prints that resulted from the programs constitute Arms' largest series of prints, the *Demonstration Series*.

Arms' demonstrations must have been fascinating and memorable events, judging from descriptions published by Carl Zigrosser and Arms' printmaking peer, Samuel Chamberlain. Zigrosser described one of these "truly amazing performances:"

*In the space of an hour or two he will demonstrate to his audience
the entire process of etching from bare copper to finished proof,
talking every second of the time even while drawing with his right
or left hand and performing the most intricate operations, giving
a running history of the art, the flavor of its great practitioners, its
purpose and spirit, and the key to its intelligent appreciation. It is a
dramatic performance of a rare kind, with local color, instruction,*

humor, and a dramatic element of suspense that keeps even the most informed listener on the edge of his seat until the demonstration is brought to a triumphant close.[5]

Chamberlain's comments on Arms' one hundredth demonstration confirms Zigrosser's impression:

> *This is an amazing performance in which [Arms] follows all the steps of making a plate—grounding the copper surface, needling the picture (casually drawing with both hands), biting in acid and pulling a finished proof—all in one tense sitting, while carrying on a stentorian monologue and apparently not once stopping for breath.*[6]

Most of the plates in the *Demonstration Series* depict architectural imagery and street scenes derived from Arms' trips to Europe and Mexico. French and Italian subjects fill the plates of the 1920s and 30s; English subjects appear in the late 30s and run through the 40s, the years that Arms developed his *English Series*. Although the *Mexican Series* is composed of only two plates, Arms used three different Mexican subjects for his demonstrations in 1940, the year he traveled there. Arms selected a Mexican view for the demonstration he conducted for NBC in July of that year. The Academy's impression of that plate, *Shadows in Mexico (Sketch)*, 1940 (F.340A, fig. 50), like the majority of prints from his *Demonstration Series*, bears an inscription the artist wrote in his careful script: "Sketch, Shadows in Mexico—Impression from Demonstration Plate etched for television broadcast of 'How to Make an Etching' at studios of National Broadcasting Company, N.Y.C., July 26, 1940." Arms was especially careful to record on the plates or their impressions where and when the demonstration took place; he often even noted the length of time the program took. On the plate for *The Grolier Club Library (Sketch)*, 1941 (F.353, fig. 51), Arms noted: "Demonstration plate, drawn, etched, and printed, in a little over two hour's [*sic*], at the Grolier Club, New York City, on the evening of March 9, 1941."

The subjects of other plates in the *Demonstration Series* are sometimes related to the site of the demonstration itself. When Arms was in Toronto, he etched the Gothic-Revival tower at the center of Canada's Parliament Building in Ottawa; in New York he needled the library of the Grolier Club for the demonstration he conducted there. At the World's Fair, he rendered exposition structures on three different occasions.[7] Each time Arms made a five-minute sketch in the fairgrounds and then conducted the demonstration before audiences of several hundred people.[8]

Although it was not unusual for Arms to spend over one thousand hours on a major plate, most demonstration prints, such as the plate etched at the Grolier Club, *The Grolier Club Library (Sketch)*, were created in approximately two hours. Arms' demonstration plates stand apart from the works in the major series such as the *French Church Series* and *Italian Series* because of their sketchier, more schematic linework. In about two hours, Arms was able to block in the basic composition, but could not take it to the same level of clarity and precision that characterize the works discussed in earlier chapters. Contour lines and simple shading not only provide the foundation for works in the *Demonstration Series*, they also underlie the creation of memorable experiences for the public, especially since impressions were distributed to the audience.[9] Perhaps because of its abstract boldness, *The Grolier Club Library (Sketch)* is one of the most striking images in the series. Symmetrical geometric patterning is oriented around the

insistent diagonals of the design's one-point perspective, creating an image of movement and syncopation.

If Arms' demonstrations promoted the cause of printmaking by demystifying the complexities of the etching process, his writings supported the same cause but from different perspectives. Arms' *Handbook of Print Making and Print Makers*, written in language appropriate for the lay reader and published in 1934, remains one of the few texts that covers the history of European and American printmaking from the fifteenth century up to its date of publication.[10] Arms also devoted significant time to writing articles on a variety of topics, including exhibition reviews and discussions of printmakers and their work, print collecting, and the history of printmaking. Articles by Arms appeared in many of the major art publications of the period such as *The Print Collector's Quarterly*, *Print*, *Art News*, and *The Art Digest*.[11]

In addition to preparing articles for those magazines, Arms also served as a contributing editor for *Print*, a publication which specialized in the graphic arts. Beginning with its inaugural issue in 1940, Arms selected an engraver or etcher about whom he wrote a brief article and with which he published a reproduction of a print. In view of Arms' own predilection for architectural subjects in general and Charles Meryon in particular, it is no surprise that the first essay celebrates the work of that late nineteenth-century French master.[12]

The other articles Arms wrote and the sentiments he articulated promoted among the general public the recognition that printmaking is a valid means of artistic expression and a necessary part of daily and national life. Arms' other essays often presented his belief that prints are spiritually fulfilling and enrich our sense of humanity. In "By-Paths in Print Collecting," Arms stated his most fundamental consideration of prints: "To me a print [is] a piece of an artist's self, born of love and inspiration, rich in knowledge and beauty, by which I might become happier and better—incapable of measurement by any monetary yardstick."[13] Arms commented further in the first issue of *Print*:

> *It is the firm belief of the editor that prints and drawings are human documents and that the greatest pleasure and profit to be derived from the study of them lies in the warm and human relationship established by such study between artist and student.*[14]

Arms again approached the same theme in an article that introduced in the same issue of *Print* his profiles of individual printmakers and prints:

> *For each and every one of us there exist, somewhere in the vast field of prints, certain pieces of paper on which certain artists have lavished loving labor through the medium of copper, wood, or stone, in black and white or in color, to which we immediately respond, whose message stimulates our imagination, or recalls to us scenes and people and events that interest us; which, in short, give us help and encouragement and inspiration, and satisfy those inner cravings, common to all men, which are of the spirit....Either in calm or storm [one can turn to prints] for spiritual refreshment and rejuvenation, for intellectual stimulus and emotional enjoyment, [they are] a veritable ever-present help in time of need.*[15]

Titles such as "The Meaning of Prints," "By-Paths in Print Collecting, French Nineteenth Century Prints—Part 1," and "Perplexing Questions and Pertinent Answers [about Prints and Print Collecting]" suggest the topics Arms discussed, hoping to make prints understandable and print collecting desirable.[16] Arms encouraged print collecting by looking beyond the role of prints as sources of personal enjoyment. He indicated that ownership of prints not only provides satisfactory aesthetic experiences, it serves a function as well: "You will be a happier and more useful member of society if you surround yourself with as many beautiful things as you can afford to possess."[17]

Arms also appealed to his readers' patriotism by stressing the importance of artistic expression and understanding in the growth of a nation:

> *Art is <u>not</u> a luxury and <u>it is</u> a necessity—something which the older countries have known for centuries but which we Americans, with all our pride in our progressive tendencies, are only just beginning to find out....Aesthetic appreciation is just as essential in the growth and evolution of a country as is scientific knowledge and industrial development—just as necessary to that country's ultimate attainment of a broad and cultured civilization which will enable it to write its name large across the pages of history.*[18]

Arms' activities in support of printmaking also took place behind the scenes with

extensive service as society founder, board and committee member, juror, and exhibition curator. The National Academy of Design elected Arms an Associate in 1930 and then Academician in 1933. Arms acted in a variety of capacities for the Academy, including First Vice President.[19] Early in his career Arms was also elected a member of the Brooklyn Society of Etchers, one of the oldest and most esteemed printmaking societies in the nation. He served as secretary and president of it and president of its successor organizations, The Society of American Etchers; The Society of American Etchers, Gravers, Lithographers and Woodcutters; and, as it is known today, The Society of American Graphic Artists.[20] During Arms' tenure the organization grew from one focused exclusively on etching to one open to printmakers of diverse media. The change of the organization's name from The Society of American Etchers to The Society of American Etchers, Gravers, Lithographers and Woodcutters reflects Arms' commitment to serve the growing diversity of American printmaking and be the most "representative" society possible.[21]

Arms was president of the Society of American Etchers for more than thirty years. An energetic leader, he directed the organization's annual show, wrote the introduction to its catalogue, and acted as a spokesperson-advocate on affairs affecting American printmakers. Arms also was an outspoken proponent of artistic freedom of expression. He protested when the Brooklyn Museum threatened to restrict non-union artists employed in the Federal Art Project and Works Progress Administration from showing their prints in an exhibition coinciding with the 1939 New York World's Fair. On behalf of the Society of American Etchers, he sent a letter to the museum indicating:

> *keen regret [over] the introduction of any political element into an open art exhibition, and the making of an artist's right to show in any exhibition contingent upon membership in any union. The Society believes that such a policy threatens the liberty of American art by tending toward the regimentation of artists.*[22]

Arms was instrumental in the development of another printmaking organization during the late 1930s and early 40s. The International Congress of Engraving held in Paris in 1937 sparked in Europe the formation of several "National Committees" devoted to promoting the cause of the graphic arts. Arms was asked to organize such a body in the United States, a body that would "foster the interests of contemporary printmaking in this country and to serve as a clearing house in matters pertaining to the international exchange of print exhibitions," which he undertook. In 1941 Arms founded with Ernest D. Roth, Stow Wengenroth, Aline Kistler, Harry T. Peters, and Otto M. Torrington the American National Committee of Engraving; he also became the organization's first president.[23]

Before the Committee became inactive during World War II, Arms directed among other projects its first exchange exhibition, *Fifty Prints from Hawaii*.[24] Working with the Honolulu Printmakers, Huc-Mazlet Luquiens, and the Honolulu Academy of Arts' first curator of prints, Alice Poole, prints by Honolulu printmakers traveled under the auspices of the American National Committee of Engraving to presentations at the New York World's Fair in 1940 and then to museums in Boston, Tulsa, Manchester, New Hampshire, and Albany, NY. In exchange, *Fifty Prints from the Mainland* appeared at the Honolulu Academy of Arts and the Maui Art Center at the Kahului fairgrounds in October and November, 1940.[25] Arms arranged other exhibitions of prints from Mexico, Britain, and Uruguay which appeared in numerous institutions in the United States in 1940 and 1941.[26]

Arms also committed himself to the organization, presentation, and circulation of exhibitions of American prints in the United States and abroad other than those sponsored under the aegis of the American National Committee of Engraving. He served on the jury for international exhibitions of American graphic art presented in Paris at the Bibliothèque Nationale and London at the Victoria and Albert Museum in 1928 and 1929, respectively; he was part of the committee responsible for assembling an American exhibition at the Paris International Exposition in 1937 and worked with New York's Grand Central Art Galleries, the National Academy of Design, and the Society of American Etchers in assembling exhibitions of American graphic art for the Venice Biennale in 1938 and then again in 1940. These efforts were followed by the organization of a goodwill exhibition sent to England in 1944 which was sponsored by Artists for Victory, an American wartime artist organization.[27]

As if these obligations were not enough, Arms worked with federal and local government agencies, such as the Works Progress Administration, in various advisory capacities. Of all his commitments involving speaking, writing, consulting, society work, and exhibition organization, Arms probably most enjoyed his stint as the first member/ consultant of the Library of Congress' Pennell Committee, the body responsible for oversight of the Pennell Fund. Arms accepted an invitation to join the committee on its founding in 1937 and remained on it until his death in 1953.

Joseph Pennell provided that on the death of his wife, his estate, including his own prints and drawings, collection of Whistleriana, and collection of prints by nineteenth- and twentieth-century American and European artists, devolved on the Library of Congress in Washington, D.C. He also established the Pennell Fund, an endowment with which the Library was to purchase additional Whistleriana and "original prints by modern artists of any nationality living or who have produced work within the last one hundred years, the prints so purchased to be of the greatest excellence only."[28] Pennell's will stipulated that the prints be selected by a committee of three members, the Chief of the Library's Fine Arts Division (now Prints and Photographs Division) and two prominent printmakers, one etcher and one lithographer, to be approved by the director of the National Gallery of Art (now National Museum of American Art) and the Corcoran Gallery of Art.[29]

After Pennell's wife died in 1936, the first Pennell Committee formed the following year led by Chief, Division of Fine Arts, Leicester B. Holland, Arms as the etcher of note, and Stow Wengenroth as the lithographer.[30] Meeting several times a year in New York City, the committee examined prints, considered the Library's holdings, and selected prints to purchase. Arms took his responsibility seriously and strove to diversify the collection. One of his first actions as a committee member was to form a list of more than one hundred contemporary printmakers whom he felt should be represented under the terms of the Pennell Bequest. The list covers a broad spectrum of printmaking, identifying artists, men and women alike, of different backgrounds working in various media and diverse styles. Names such as Grace Albee, Peggy Bacon, Isabel Bishop, Paul Cadmus, Stuart Davis, Wanda Gág, Edward Hopper, Rockwell Kent, Yasuo Kuniyoshi, John Marin, B.J.O. Nordfeldt, Charles Sheeler, Raphael Soyer, Benton Spruance, and Abraham Walkowitz suggest the range of American printmakers and printmaking that Arms had in mind in 1937.[31] Over the years that Arms served on the committee, the Library of Congress acquired prints by many of these masters as well as European printmakers such as Henri de Toulouse-Lautrec, Pablo Picasso, and Käthe Kollwitz.[32] Under Arms' tenure, the Library of Congress acquired an impression of Guy Maccoy's *Three Trees and a Low Sky*, 1943, one of the first color screenprints to enter the collection.[33]

Arms' interest in broadening the print holdings of the Library of Congress typifies his approach to viewing the work of his peers and promoting prints as a legitimate and important means of artistic expression. During the length of his career, in lectures, interviews, exhibition organization and catalogue introductions, and articles for publication, he advanced the cause of open-minded tolerance in the consideration of all art. The concluding paragraph of his article "Self Estimate," an essay in which he discusses his work and philosophy of art, outlines his support of artistic freedom of expression with phrases that are constant refrains in his other writings:

> *I believe in no rigid definition of art, I hold with no single approach, I recognize no division of artists into groups, schools, or 'tendencies.' I may neither understand nor agree with my fellow-worker in the common field, but I demand for him the right to worship at his own particular shrine in his own particular way and to allow me to do the same.*[34]

Maintaining such an accepting attitude must have been difficult for Arms, since he realized that what he valued—craftsmanship, hard work, sincere effort, vision, and above all the search for beauty—was not important to many of his peers. Arms acknowledged this dilemma in a speech before the American Art Dealers Association:

> *My own philosophy of art is so simple that I become confused and puzzled when brought into contact with all the varying trends of thought, points of view, and interpretations of artistic creeds, that war with each other and seem to me to cloud rather than to clarify a simple issue. To love beauty and, loving it, to seek to express it— therein appears to me the function and the duty of the artist. Of course my 'modern' brethren laugh at me for this and point out that such a belief is entirely demoded, that it belongs to another*

day, and is quite out of step with the fast moving and sophisticated life of our time.[35]

Arms expressed his disapproval of progressive tendencies by referring to this "time when the craze for something new in art, the quest of the 'ism,' has given birth to so much that is restlessly and superficially clever."[36] Although Arms did not name names or otherwise identify the artists whose work he did not enjoy, he elaborated generally on his concerns in an article in which, after praising the pictorially rendered architectural prints of Ernest Roth, he commented:

> *Haste, lack of thoroughness, neglect of craftsmanship, and an effort to achieve effect at the expense of mastery of hard won fundamentals, are all too characteristic of our art expression....It is all very well to dwell upon self expression and the divine fire of inspiration, but no expression that does not stand firmly on the great basic essentials of all art, that is not regulated by strict discipline and developed by unremitting toil and self sacrifice, that is not as completely sincere as it is free and personal, and that does not take into account that body of human experience beside which the effort of the individual, however brilliant, is but a very minor quantity, can be one of the first order.*[37]

Despite Arms' fundamental disagreement with the conceptual framework found in the work of many of his more progressive contemporaries, he nonetheless protected their right to freedom of expression and the right of all artists to equal respect. Arms realized that the formally organized institutions dedicated to printmaking, such as the Society of American Graphic Artists, were essentially conservative and unreceptive to modernist expression. From his position of power and esteem within the administrative ranks of these organizations, he attempted to broaden the attitudes of his peers and develop a community more accepting of changing aesthetic perspectives. Arms took advantage of every opportunity, whether it be in the organization of a show or by spoken and written word, whether it be in an exhibition review, catalogue introduction, independent article, or speech, to urge tolerance of all modes of artistic expression. In the same previously quoted speech before the American Art Dealers Association, Arms stood firm:

> *Because we artists are all workers in this field of beauty, have we not the same wish in common, the same goal in sight, the same fundamental beliefs?...Because my friend sees and feels and expresses himself differently,...is he thereby 'wrong,' or am I? Does not the most radical 'modern' respond to the same emotional and intellectual forces that move the most dyed-in-the-wool 'conservative,' and is not the expression of each governed by exactly the same fundamental laws?...Each of us feels differently, of course, and each differently expresses himself because he is an individual, but the great underlying thought is the same and all the 'isms' and 'ists' in our world cannot change it one whit....A great tradition builds itself up through the ages, made up of all the individual contributions of all true artists, great and small. Each one takes that which has been handed to him;*

from it he extracts what he best can use; to it he adds his little con-
tribution; and upon it he marks the stamps of his own individuali-
ty....What does it matter whether he is called 'radical' or 'old hat;'
the great tradition goes on, enriched in each age by the labor and
devotion of countless men.[38]

As Arms' statement before the American Art Dealers Association suggests, he also spoke out against the tendency of exhibition organizers and others involved with print-making affairs to polarize printmakers by dividing them into two formally designated categories, "conservative" and "modern." This development was led by the American Institute of Graphic Arts when it implemented in 1932 a new "ratio system" designed to make the annual *The Fifty Prints of the Year* exhibitions as "representative of con-temporary tendencies as possible." According to the new policy, two jurors, one responsible for the "conservative" submissions and the other for the "modern," would classify the entries prior to jurying as either "modern" or "conservative." The pro-portionate breakdown of conservative to modern prints within the entire entry pool would determine the number of modern prints the modern juror could select out of the exhibition's total of fifty prints and the percentage of conservative prints that the conservative juror could choose.[39]

In principle, Arms agreed with the attempt of the *Fifty Prints* exhibition organizers to present "representative" exhibitions; it was with the method that he was in absolute disagreement. In his address before the American Art Dealers Association, Arms railed against what he perceived to be the artificial categorization of artists' work: "Does it matter much, be a man sincere, what you call him? What do 'modern' and 'con-servative' mean—are they anything more than handles by which to pick up men's names and place a false estimate upon men's values?"[40] Another exhibition review by Arms reflects his concern that the categorization of printmakers was unproductive, creating divisiveness within the printmaking community rather than mutual support and appreciation. He commented:

The print world is unhappily afflicted with jealousies, rivalries,
and the separation of artists into groups representing phases,
tendencies, isms, the moderns and conservatives, the progressives,
realists, abstractionists, independents, radicals....Instead of har-
mony in the pursuit of beauty, there is opposition, recrimination,
misunderstanding.[41]

In deed as well as by word, Arms attempted to liberalize the conservative strong-hold of the printmaking establishment. With unflagging commitment he politicked his way to more "representative" or progressively inclusive exhibitions. Arms described what he wished to foster at the Society of American Graphic Artists in a letter to Rockwell Kent; he hoped to create a:

real exhibition of real American prints with no prejudice in
favor of any 'school' or 'tendency' but with every effort made
to have it contain an example of the work of every sincere and
significant American print maker, irrespective of whether he calls
himself 'modern,' 'conservative' or anything else.[42]

Achieving a representative show was important to Arms because he believed that "only in this way can the true interest in American art be conserved and the graphic artists be brought together on the common ground of mutual understanding, respect, and cooperation."[43]

Arms' voluminous correspondence with Kent and other printmakers of all "varying trends of thought, points of view, and interpretations of artistic creeds" reveal Arms' efforts to persuade them to submit prints to exhibitions that he was directing, despite their frustration over the conservative nature of the institutional body. A series of letters in 1935 and 1936 between Arms and the printmaker Harry Wickey provides insights into Arms' effort to broaden representation of more progressive artists in the annual shows of the Society of American Graphic Artists.[44] Arms was disturbed that Wickey had withdrawn his membership in the Society and did not submit prints for jurying. In addition to requesting that Wickey reconsider his decision, Arms asked Wickey to send him the names of artists whom Wickey believed should be included—Arms wished to work with them and the Society so that their prints would appear in and strengthen the annual exhibitions. Arms wrote:

> *it will be utterly impossible to continue the drive for a wider*
> *inclusion of differing viewpoints unless the jury each year is faced*
> *with material that will issue a challenge. If those whose work is*
> *significant withdraw and fail to send in their prints, there can*
> *be no possible change in selection, for there will be no new challenge*
> *to bring about a fresh evaluation and judgment.*[45]

Arms realized that any exhibition could only be as "representative" or progressive as the artwork proposed for inclusion.

Arms' attempt to buck the more conservative members of the Society and ensure broader representation did not go unnoted nor unappreciated. Wickey himself acknowledged that, "Arms was doing his utmost to present exhibitions that were truly representative...and [I] am grateful to him for the immense energy he has expended in behalf of...printmaking in America."[46]

Arms' achievements and contributions as both printmaker and advocate were well recognized nationally and internationally. Over the years his prints garnered ninety awards in a variety of exhibitions across the country.[47] Arms also received an impressive number of personal honors of national and international importance. The American Art Dealers Association awarded him a Gold Medal in 1934; and the American Institute of Architects acknowledged his work by presenting him with a Fine Arts Medal for Etching (Gold) in 1945. Wesleyan University, Princeton University, and Hobart College commemorated Arms' contributions to their institutions by presenting him with honorary degrees; the first two bestowed on him Master of Arts degrees, the latter a Doctor of Letters degree.[48] Two major honors marked 1947, when Arms was elected Member of the American Academy of Arts and Letters, one of the nation's most distinguished institutions dedicated to the support of literature, music, and art; he also became a Fellow in Perpetuity, Ex Officio, of New York's Metropolitan Museum of Art. In 1933, the same year that he was elected Academician of the National Academy of Design, Arms received the first of his international citations; he became a Chevalier in France's Legion of Honor, one of the most prestigious merit societies in the world. The Italian State Tourist Department in Rome presented Arms and his wife Dorothy with a Silver Medal in 1934, and in 1937 he received a Gold Medal from the Paris International Exposition. Two years before his death in 1953 Arms achieved the rank of Officer in the Legion of Honor of France, an honor that no doubt provided him with enormous satisfaction after so many years devoted to the visual expression of that nation's glorious Gothic architectural heritage.[49]

Arms' death in 1953 was marked by several exhibitions as well as obituaries published in newspapers and "appreciations" in art magazines.[50] Kennedy Galleries in New York held a memorial show in early 1954 featuring impressions of some of his finest work drawn from the length of his career; Grand Central Art Galleries also presented a memorial exhibition of prints and preparatory drawings.[51] It is the activities and words of his peers, however, about whom Arms cared deeply and whose regard affected him profoundly, that probably speak best to the importance of his work and activities.

In 1955 the Society of American Graphic Artists presented to the Metropolitan Museum of Art the John Taylor Arms Memorial Collection. The collection is composed of works created by members of the Society and donated by them in Arms' honor. The collection of 212 prints by 207 members—of all "creeds," "tendencies," and "standards"—was exhibited at the museum at the time of its formal presentation in honor of Arms and his wife.[52] Samuel Chamberlain, Jean Charlot, Paul Landacre, Armin Landeck, Julius Lankes, Doel Reed, and Stow Wengenroth are among the many who participated.[53]

High accolades for Arms appeared in published form, such as in *Print*, the magazine for which Arms was a contributing editor. William J. Schaldach, Arms' friend and fellow printmaker, noted that Arms "was unquestionably *the world's greatest virtuoso of the bitten line.*"[54] Albert Reese of Kennedy Galleries wrote:

> *Not only is his technical virtuosity extraordinary, but his understanding and reverence for the great have made him the most eloquent exponent of the graphic arts in our time....Arms has probably done more than anyone else to keep printmaking a living and a vital force in American art.*[55]

Notes of appreciation poured in to Lynd Ward, the new president of the Society of American Graphic Artists, after he announced Arms' death to the membership. Roi Partridge wrote:

> *No one in this country, except possibly Berthe E. Jaques, has done as much for etchers and etching as Arms did. He was outstanding as a kindly, helpful man who reached out beyond himself to touch and influence the lives of others....There is no one who can replace him in the graphic arts world of today.*[56]

John Winkler commented on Arms' etching and his work for the Society of American Graphic Artists:

> *John Taylor Arms will live on and on and future generations centuries from now will marvel at his work. That is more than will be our share....[His printmaking] stands firmly on its own ground, independent of any art movements or fluctuations in tastes, and like the Pyramids, it will outlast almost anything. As a friend and man he fully matched his superb work and I can well comprehend the loss to the Society to which he was so wholeheartedly devoted.*[57]

Although writing about Arms years before his death, Samuel Chamberlain's words published in an article aptly titled "John Taylor Arms...Phenomenon" provide the best closing on a long and productive career spent creating some of the finest prints in the United States during the first half of this century and advancing the cause of American printmaking nationally and internationally. With humor and affection, Chamberlain itemized some of Arms' accomplishments and activities:

> *John Arms is an exception among etchers. No other American printmaker has reached so wide an audience. None knows so many of his fellow etchers by their first names. No five of them have put so much devoted labor into the Cause of Etching. He belongs to a bewildering list of print societies. Anything which brings art to the common man, particularly the etcher's art, has his immediate support. Any young etcher about to embark on his career has a firm potential friend in him. He serves on endless committees and juries, arranges countless exhibitions and writes more letters than a Congressman up for reelection. And in the meantime he manages to execute the most minutely-etched plates ever attempted in American printmaking.*[58]

Chamberlain grappled with the difficulty of synopsizing such an extraordinary career but was able to approach the task directly and again with understanding and humor:

> *In writing about John Taylor Arms one is immediately tempted to indulge in sweeping superlatives—to assert that he has achieved the greatest technical mastery of etching, drawn the most Gothic churches, given the most demonstrations, run more societies, written more articles, befriended more etchers and, in general, influenced American etching more than any man of his generation....Arms is a phenomenon.*[59]

1. Fletcher, *John Taylor Arms, A Man for All Time*, p. 291.
2. Bassham, *John Taylor Arms*, p. 31.
3. *Buckingham "To F.L.M.G." (Sketch)*, 1942 (F.367) was etched at the Kansas City Art Institute on March 19, 1942, and *Parliament Building, Ottawa, Canada (Sketch)*, 1941 (F.359) was etched for Canadian International Business Machines, Inc., at the Royal York Hotel in Toronto on September 2, 1941.
4. Samuel Chamberlain, "John Taylor Arms...Phenomenon," *Print* 1, no. 4 (Mar. 1941), p. 43.
5. Zigrosser, *The Artist in America*, p. 30.
6. Chamberlain, "John Taylor Arms...Phenomenon," p. 43.
7. See, for example, *Parliament Building, Ottawa, Canada (Sketch)*, 1941 (F.359); *New York World's Fair, Bell Telephone Building (Sketch)*, 1939 (F.326).
8. "Demonstrations at Art Exhibition Fascinate World's Fair Visitors," *New York World Telegram*, Jul. 15, 1939, John Taylor Arms vertical file, Prints Division, New York Public Library.
9. Kropfl, "A Catalogue of the Work of John Taylor Arms," p. 13.
10. John Taylor Arms, *Handbook of Print Making and Print Makers* (New York: The Macmillan Company, 1934).
11. See, for instance, the following articles by Arms: "The Meaning of Prints," *The Print Collector's Quarterly* 29, no. 3 (Nov. 1948), pp. 5–11; "Printmakers' Processes and a Militant Show," *Art News* 42, no. 10 (Oct. 1–14, 1943), pp. 8–15, 32; "Among the Print Makers, Old and Modern, John Taylor Arms Reviews Academy's Print Show for Art Digest," *The Art Digest* 5, no. 5 (Dec. 1, 1930), pp. 24–25, 3–4; "Childe Hassam, Etcher of Light," *Prints* 4, no. 1 (November 1933), frontispiece, pp. 1–12.

12. John Taylor Arms, "One Hundred Masterpieces of Print Making: No. 1: *La Morgue* by Charles Meryon," *Print* 1, no. 1 (June 1940), pp. 96–97.

13. John Taylor Arms, "By-Paths in Print Collecting, French Nineteenth Century Prints—Part I," *Prints* 7, no. 4 (Apr. 1937), pp. 194–195.

14. John Taylor Arms, "Prints and Print Making," *Print* 1, no. 1 (June 1940), p. 91.

15. John Taylor Arms, "One Hundred Masterpieces of Print Making," *Print* 1, no. 1 (June 1940), p. 95.

16. Arms wrote the first two articles, "The Meaning of Prints," *The Print Collector's Quarterly* 29, no. 3 (Nov. 1948), pp. 5–11; "By-Paths in Print Collecting, French Nineteenth Century Prints—Part I," *Prints* 7, no. 4 (Apr. 1937), pp. 194–203. The third article was written in collaboration with J.H. Bender, "Perplexing Questions and Pertinent Answers," *The Print Collector's Quarterly* 28, no. 4 (Dec. 1941), pp. 418–441.

17. John Taylor Arms, "Etchings and the Brooklyn Society of Etchers," *The Brooklyn Museum Quarterly* 18, no. 2 (Apr. 1931), p. 59.

18. *Ibid.*, p. 57.

19. Kropfl, "A Catalogue of the Work of John Taylor Arms," p. 23.

20. *Ibid.*, pp. 22–23.

21. Letter from John Taylor Arms to Fellow Member [Blanche McVeigh], dated New York [City], The Society of American Etchers, Inc., Feb. 1, 1947 (Blanche McVeigh Papers, 1684:347, AAA).

22. Letter from John Taylor Arms to Director, Brooklyn Institute of Arts and Sciences, Brooklyn Museum [copy], dated Feb. 11, 1939 (Brooklyn Museum Papers, BR-21:735, AAA).

23. The Archives of American Art possesses correspondence between Arms and individuals associated with printmaking in the United States which helps trace the organization of the American National Committee of Engraving. See, for example, letter from Arms to Leila Mechlin, dated New York City, Feb. 22, 1939 (Philadelphia Archives of American Art, Philadelphia Museum of Art, P10:43, AAA) and letter from Arms to Carl Zigrosser, dated New York [City], American National Committee of Engraving, Apr. 8, 1941 (Carl Zigrosser Papers, 4613:722, AAA). See also Kropfl, "A Catalogue of the Work of John Taylor Arms," p. 24.

24. Kropfl, "A Catalogue of the Work of John Taylor Arms," p. 24.

25. "Report of Activities of the National Committee of Engraving, to April 9, 1941," pp. 1–2 (Carl Zigrosser Papers, 4613:723, AAA).

26. *Ibid.*, pp. 1–4 (4613:723–725).

27. Kropfl, "A Catalogue of the Work of John Taylor Arms," pp. 26–27.

28. Quoted in Ingrid Maar, "The Pennell Legacy, Two Centuries of Printmaking," in *The Pennell Legacy, Two Centuries of Printmaking*, exh. cat. (Washington, D.C.: Library of Congress, 1983), [p.1].

29. Alan Fern, "Introduction," in *American Prints in the Library of Congress, A Catalog of the Collection* (Baltimore and London: The Johns Hopkins Press, 1970), p. xii.

30. Correspondence between Arms and Holland provides some background information on the formation of the committee. Not formally catalogued at the time of this text's publication, the letters reside in the Prints and Photographs Division of the Library of Congress in a file marked "Arms, John Taylor" and an envelope labeled "Pennell Fund Committee, Correspondence re: original appointments of J[ohn] T[aylor] A[rms] and S[tow] W[engenroth]."

31. *Ibid.*

32. "Pennell Fund Acquisitions of the 1930s" and "Pennell Fund Acquisitions of the 1940s" in *The Pennell Legacy, Two Centuries of Printmaking*, [pp. 8–9].

33. Watrous, *A Century of American Printmaking*, pp. 104, 107.

34. Arms, "Self Estimate," p. 12.

35. "Arms, Receiving Art Dealers Medal, Makes a Plea for Tolerance," *The Art Digest* 8, no. 16 (May 15, 1934), p. 32.

36. Arms, "Among the Print Makers, Old and Modern," p. 25.

37. John Taylor Arms, "Ernest D. Roth, Etcher," *The Print Collector's Quarterly* 25, no. 1 (Feb. 1938), p. 37.

38. "Arms, Receiving Art Dealers Medal," *The Art Digest*, p. 32.

39. "Nation's Print Makers 58 Percent Conservative, Year's '50' Reveal," *The Art Digest* 6, no. 11 (Mar. 1, 1932), p. 3.

40. "Arms, Receiving Art Dealers Medal," *The Art Digest*, p. 32. Arms was actually the juror of the "conservative" print section of *The Fifty Prints of the Year* exhibition of 1932. Perhaps it was this experience of pigeonholing artists as "conservative" or "modern" that led Arms to his dissatisfaction with the use of such "handles." Max Weber was the juror for the "modern" section that year.

41. John Taylor Arms, "An Exhibition That Came True," *Prints* 6, no. 5 (June 1936), p. 251.

42. Letter from John Taylor Arms to Rockwell Kent, dated New York City, Jan. 21, 1937 (Carl Zigrosser Papers, 4613:674, AAA).

43. *Ibid.*

44. See correspondence between Arms and Wickey dated 1935 and 1936 (Harry Wickey Papers, 3683: 242–254, AAA). See in particular letter from Arms to Wickey, dated Fairfield, CT, Jan. 30, 1936 (3683: 249–250).

45. Letter from John Taylor Arms to Harry Wickey, dated New York City, Oct. 21, 1936 (Harry Wickey Papers, 3683:254, AAA).

46. Quoted in Watrous, *A Century of American Printmaking*, p. 81.

47. Pelletier, "John Taylor Arms, His World and Work," pp. 103–108.

48. Among other activities, Arms etched six plates depicting different buildings on the Princeton campus for a university portfolio; he was a visiting lecturer on graphic art at Wesleyan University in 1938 and 1939; over the years he presented numerous etching demonstrations for each institution.

49. Pelletier, "John Taylor Arms, His World and Work," p. 109.

50. See "John Taylor Arms, Artist, Dies at 66," *New York Times*, Oct. 15, 1953; "John Taylor Arms, 66, American Etcher, Dead," *New York Herald Tribune*, Oct. 15, 1953; William J. Schaldach, "John Taylor Arms, 1887–1953, An Appreciation," *Print* 8, no. 5 (Feb.–Mar. 1954), pp. viii–ix; and Arthur W. Heintzelman, "John Taylor Arms: In Memoriam," *The Boston Public Library Quarterly* 6, no. 4 (Oct. 1954), pp. 229–234.

51. See *Memorial Exhibition, John Taylor Arms (1887–1953)*, exh. cat. (New York: Kennedy Galleries, Inc., 1954).

52. The Metropolitan Museum of Art press release headed "John Taylor Arms Memorial Collection of Prints Shown for First Time at Metropolitan; 207 Contemporary American Graphic Artists Represented in Exhibit Opening Tomorrow," dated New York City, Sept. 17, 1955 (Lynd Ward Papers, 4468:286, AAA).

53. See Lynd Ward Papers, roll 4467, AAA, for voluminous correspondence between Ward and the Society of American Graphic Artists membership documenting the various donations.

54. Schaldach, "John Taylor Arms, 1887–1953," p. viii.

55. Quoted in Heintzelman, "John Taylor Arms: In Memoriam," p. 229.

56. Letter from Roi Partridge to Society of American Etchers, dated Oakland, CA, Oct. 22, 1953 (Lynd Ward Papers, 4467:119, AAA).

57. Letter from John W. Winkler to The Council of the Society of Graphic Artists, Inc., dated Berkeley, CA, Nov. 4, 1953 (Lynd Ward Papers, 4467:131–132, AAA).

58. Chamberlain, "John Taylor Arms…Phenomenon," p. 43.

59. *Ibid.*, p. 43.

Note to the Reader

In the catalogue entries below, the title of each print is followed by its date of publication; at times the year of publication post-dates the year inscribed on the plate. "Fletcher" numbers refer to William Dolan Fletcher's catalogue raisonné, *John Taylor Arms, A Man for All Time, The Artist and His Work* (The Sign of the Arrow, 1982); "Arms" numbers refer to the unpublished typescript catalogue organized by John Taylor Arms and Dorothy Noyes Arms, "Descriptive Catalogue of the Work of John Taylor Arms" in the Prints Division of the New York Public Library. Alternate titles and publication year adhere to those recorded in Fletcher's catalogue raisonné. All margin inscriptions are in pencil unless otherwise noted, and all paper colors are neutral cream, off-white, etc. unless otherwise cited. The punctuation recorded in the pencil and etched inscriptions reflects as closely as possible that on the Academy's impressions. Slashes preceded and followed by a space appearing in inscriptions refer to line breaks. Identification of paper weights is, by necessity, approximate. Information regarding commissions, prizes, publication history, edition size, state, and printers which are recorded in Fletcher's catalogue raisonné are not included unless expressly identified on the impression by inscription or corroborated by other evidence. (For instance, it is assumed that only David Strang would be Arms' printer for impressions on paper with a "David Strang" watermark.) Series designations follow the lists published in S. William Pelletier's "John Taylor Arms, His World and Work," *Georgia Museum of Art Bulletin* 17 (1993), pp. 110–124. Honolulu Academy of Arts accession numbers appear at the end of each entry. Abbreviations used are as follows: lower right=l.r.; lower center=l.c.; lower left=l.l.; upper right=u.r.; upper left=u.l.; Eliza Lefferts and Charles Montague Cooke, Jr. Collection=ELC and CMC.

Sunlight and Shadow, 1915
Also called *Old Lisieux Gable* and
La Lumière des Ombres
Fletcher 1; Arms 1
Etching printed on lightweight antique laid paper
5^{15}/$_{16}$ x 4 in. (15.1 x 10.2 cm)
Signed and dated l.r. margin: John Taylor Arms, 1915; titled and inscribed l.l. margin: Sunlight and Shadow / First published plate. 1915; monogram stamped in ink l.c. margin: JTA [intertwined]; inscribed, signed, and dated l.r. margin: To Vicky, from John—1952
Gable Series #1
Gift of Richard H. and Helen T. Hagemeyer, 1989 (20,606)

Lisieux: Gable in the Grande Rue, 1916
Also called *A Gable in the Grande Rue, Lisieux* and *La Lucarne: Grande Rue de Lisieux*
Fletcher 3; Arms 3
Etching printed on medium-weight laid paper
5^{7}/$_{16}$ x 3 in. (13.8 x 7.6 cm)
Signed l.r. margin: John Taylor Arms—
Gable Series #2
Gift of Richard H. and Helen T. Hagemeyer, 1991 (21,151)

Out of My Window, 1916
Also called *Vista, My Own* and *De Ma Fenêtre*
Fletcher 4; Arms 4
Etching printed with chine collé on heavyweight wove paper
7^{7}/$_{8}$ x 6 in. (20.0 x 15.2 cm)
Signed and dated l.r. margin: John Taylor Arms—1916
New York Series #2
Blind stamp: ELC and CMC
Gift of Eliza Lefferts and Charles Montague Cooke, Jr., 1941 (11,697)

Veterans, 1916
Also called *Silent Witnesses*
Fletcher 6; Arms 6
Etching printed with chine collé on heavyweight wove paper
6^{1}/$_{16}$ x 3^{15}/$_{16}$ in. (15.4 x 10.0 cm)
Signed l.r. margin: John Taylor Arms
Gable Series #3
Blind stamp: ELC and CMC
Gift of Eliza Lefferts and Charles Montague Cooke, Jr., 1927 (6525)

The Oldest Settler, Bayeux, France, 1917
Also called *P. Labbe, Restauranteur* and *Bayeux*
Fletcher 13; Arms 11
Etching printed on medium-weight laid paper
15^{3}/$_{8}$ x 9^{5}/$_{8}$ in. (39.1 x 24.4 cm)
Signed l.r. margin: John Taylor Arms; titled, inscribed, and signed with an initial l.l. margin: The Oldest Settler, Bayeux / One of my earliest plates—the eleventh recorded. Date —1917 I hope there has been some improvement since this one!—J.; inscribed, signed, and dated l.l. margin: To my friend Helen Loggis, / John Taylor Arms 1938
Gift of Richard H. and Helen T. Hagemeyer, 1993 (25,097)

New York from Staten Island Ferry, 1917
Also called *New York Skyline*
Fletcher 14; Arms 12
Drypoint printed on medium-weight laid paper
1^{1}/$_{2}$ x 3^{15}/$_{16}$ in. (3.8 x 10.0 cm)
22/35
Signed l.r. margin: John Taylor Arms—; titled and inscribed l.l. margin: New York from the Staten Island Ferry (drypoint)
Miniature Series #1; New York Series #3
Blind stamp: ELC and CMC
Gift of Eliza Lefferts and Charles Montague Cooke, Jr., 1927 (6523)

The Sign, Au Bon Café, 1917
Also called *The Sign* and *L'Enseigne*
Fletcher 17; Arms 15
Etching printed in brown ink on heavyweight card stock
6¹¹/₁₆ x 2¹⁵/₁₆ in. (17.0 x 7.5 cm)
6/13; sixth state
Signed and dated l.r. margin: John Taylor Arms—1919; titled l.l. margin: L'Enseigne
Gift of Richard H. and Helen T. Hagemeyer, 1989 (20,607)

Piazza del Commune, Carbognano, 1919
Fletcher 18; Arms 16
Etching printed on heavyweight card stock
6¹¹/₁₆ x 11 in. (17.0 x 27.9 cm)
Artist's proof; printed by Frederick Reynolds
Signed and dated l.r. margin: John Taylor Arms—1919; inscribed, signed, and dated l.c. margin: To Fred / from / John—1920
Note: from the estate of Frederick Reynolds
Gift of Richard H. and Helen T. Hagemeyer, 1989 (20,608)

The Quiet Street, Lisieux, 1919
Also called *The Quiet Street*
Fletcher 19; Arms 17
Etching, aquatint printed on medium-weight Japanese wove paper
8³/₈ x 6¹¹/₁₆ in. (21.3 x 17.0 cm)
15/25; printed by Frederick Reynolds
Signed, dated, and inscribed l.r. margin: John Taylor Arms—1919 / Printed by Frederick Reynolds; titled l.l. margin: The Quiet Street
Aquatint Series #1
Blind stamp: ELC and CMC
Gift of Eliza Lefferts and Charles Montague Cooke, Jr., 1927 (6517)

The Quiet Street, Lisieux, 1919
Also called *The Quiet Street*
Fletcher 19; Arms 17
Etching, aquatint printed on medium-weight laid paper
8⁷/₁₆ x 6³/₄ in. (21.4 x 17.1 cm)
Artist's proof
Signed and dated l.r. margin: John T. Arms 1919
Aquatint Series #1
Gift of Richard H. and Helen T. Hagemeyer, 1989 (20,609)

Lace, Place Victor Hugo, Lisieux, 1919
Also called *Lacet, Place Victor Hugo, Lisieux*
Fletcher 20; Arms 18
Etching printed on medium-weight Japanese laid paper
7 x 9⁹/₁₆ in. (17.8 x 24.3 cm)
25/50; third state; printed by Frederick Reynolds
Signed and dated l.r. margin: John Taylor Arms—1919; titled l.l. margin: "Lace;" signed l.l. margin: Frederick Reynolds Imp.
Blind stamp: ELC and CMC
Gift of Eliza Lefferts and Charles Montague Cooke, Jr., 1927 (6522)

A Hong Kong Canal Boat, 1919
Fletcher 23; Arms 22
Etching, aquatint printed on medium-weight laid paper
8¹/₈ x 5⁵/₈ in. (20.6 x 14.3 cm)
Fourth state
Signed l.r. margin: John Taylor Arms
Aquatint Series #5

Gift of Richard H. and Helen T. Hagemeyer, 1993 (25,098)

The Harbor at Aden, 1919
Also called *Aden*
Fletcher 24; Arms 23
Etching, aquatint printed on heavyweight laid paper
4¹¹/₁₆ x 6¹³/₁₆ in. (11.9 x 17.3 cm)
14/20; fifth state
Signed and dated l.r. margin: John Taylor Arms—1919
Aquatint Series #6
Gift of Richard H. and Helen T. Hagemeyer, 1993 (25,099)

Still Waters, 1919
Fletcher 28; Arms 27
Etching, aquatint printed in color on medium-weight laid paper
6 x 4 in. (15.2 x 10.2 cm)
6/40; fourth state; printed by Frederick Reynolds
Signed and dated l.r. margin: John Taylor Arms—1919; titled l.l. margin: Still Waters; signed l.l. margin: Frederick Reynolds. Imp.
Aquatint Series #10
Gift of Richard H. and Helen T. Hagemeyer, 1991 (21,152)

Sunrise, Mont Saint-Michel, 1919
Also called *Mont Saint-Michel, Sunrise*
Fletcher 29; Arms 28
Etching, aquatint printed on heavyweight card stock
6¹/₂ x 7⁹/₁₆ in. (16.5 x 19.2 cm)
Tenth state; printed by Frederick Reynolds
Signed and dated l.r. margin: John Taylor Arms—1919
Note: from the estate of Frederick Reynolds
Aquatint Series #11
Gift of Richard H. and Helen T. Hagemeyer, 1991 (21,153)

Dol—Old Houses in La Grande Rue, 1919
Also called *Dol—La Grande Rue*
Fletcher 30; Arms 29
Etching printed in brown ink on medium-weight laid paper
7¹/₂ x 9³/₄ in. (19.1 x 24.8 cm)
12/50; fourth state; printed by Frederick Reynolds
Signed, dated, and inscribed l.r. margin: John Taylor Arms—1919 / Printed by Frederick Reynolds
Gift of Lila L. and James F. Morgan, 1983 (18,566)

Dol—Old Houses in La Grande Rue, 1919
Also called *Dol—La Grande Rue*
Fletcher 30; Arms 29
Etching printed on medium-weight laid paper
7⁷/₁₆ x 9¹¹/₁₆ in. (18.9 x 24.6 cm)
Signed l.r. margin: John Taylor Arms; titled l.l. margin: Dol, Old Houses in the Grande Rue
Gift of Richard H. and Helen T. Hagemeyer, 1991 (21,154)

A Winding Street, Mans, 1919
Also called *Mans, A Winding Street*
Fletcher 31; Arms 30
Etching printed on lightweight Japanese wove paper
1¹³/₁₆ x 5⁵/₈ in. (28.4 x 13.7 cm)
2/50; third state

Signed and dated l.r. margin: John Taylor Arms—1919; titled l.l. margin: A Winding Street, Mans; signed with initials l.r. plate: J.T.A.; inscribed, signed, and dated l.l. margin: To my friend Eugene Higgins / John Taylor Arms—1920
Gift of Richard H. and Helen T. Hagemeyer, 1989 (20,610)

Somewhere in France, 1919
Fletcher 32; Arms 31
Etching printed on medium-weight laid paper
12¹/₈ x 6 in. (30.8 x 15.2 cm)
Signed and dated l.r. margin: John Taylor Arms—1919; titled l.l. margin: "Somewhere in France;" signed with initials and dated l.r. plate: J.T.A—1919
Gift of Richard H. and Helen T. Hagemeyer, 1989 (20,611)

The Market Place, Honfleur, 1919
Also called *Ste. Catherine Belfry, Honfleur*
Fletcher 33; Arms 32
Etching printed on heavyweight wove paper
8¹/₈ x 4⁹/₁₆ in. (20.6 x 11.6 cm)
5/50; second state
Signed and dated l.r. margin: John Taylor Arms. 1919; titled l.l. margin: The Market Place, Honfleur; signed with initials and dated l.r. plate: J.T.A.—1919; inscribed, signed, and dated l.l. margin: To my friend Eugene Higgins / John Taylor Arms—1920
Gift of Richard H. and Helen T. Hagemeyer, 1989 (20,612)

Top-o'-the-World, Madrid, Maine, 1919
Fletcher 36B; Arms 35A
Etching printed on medium-weight Japanese laid paper
3⁷/₈ x 5¹/₂ in. (9.8 x 14.0 cm)
9/100
Signed and dated l.r. margin: John Taylor Arms—1919; titled l.l. margin: "Top-o'-the-World"—Madrid, Maine—
Maine Series #1
Gift of Richard H. and Helen T. Hagemeyer, 1988 (20,481)

At Chinon, 1919
Also called *Chinon*
Fletcher 39; Arms 38
Etching printed on medium-weight laid paper
2¹⁵/₁₆ x 2 in. (7.5 x 5.1 cm)
3/75
Signed and dated l.r. margin: John T. Arms—1919; titled l.l. margin: At Chinon
Demonstration Series #2; Miniature Series #3
Gift of Richard H. and Helen T. Hagemeyer, 1988 (20,482)

West Forty-Second Street, 1920
Fletcher 41; Arms 40
Etching printed on medium-weight Japanese wove paper
13¹/₈ x 10¹/₂ in. (33.3 x 26.7 cm)
26/75
Signed and dated l.r. margin: John Taylor Arms—1920—
Note: done with the assistance of Charles Cameron Clarke, partner in Arms' architectural firm
New York Series #5
Purchase, Academy Volunteers Fund, 1989 (20,545)

"S.C.'s" On Night Patrol, 1920
Also called *S.C. 151*
Fletcher 43; Arms 42
Etching, aquatint printed in blue ink on
medium-weight laid paper
3⁷⁄₈ x 10 in. (9.8 x 25.4 cm)
Signed l.r. margin: John Taylor Arms
Aquatint Series #13
Gift of Richard H. and Helen T. Hagemeyer,
1989 (20,613)

Moonlight, Number One, 1920
Also called *Sailing, Moonlight*
Fletcher 47; Arms 46
Etching, aquatint printed in blue ink on
medium-weight Japanese wove paper
7³⁄₈ x 2³⁄₈ in. (18.7 x 6.0 cm)
7/100; second state
Signed l.r. margin: John Taylor Arms—; titled
l.l. margin: Moonlight, Number One; inscribed
l.r. margin: 12⁰⁰
Aquatint Series #17
Gift of Richard H. and Helen T. Hagemeyer,
1993 (24,030)

The Butterfly, 1920
Fletcher 48; Arms 47
Etching, aquatint printed on medium-weight
laid paper
10¹⁄₄ x 7¹⁄₄ in. (26.0 x 18.4 cm)
29/75; second state; printed by Frederick
Reynolds
Signed, dated, and inscribed l.r. margin:
John Taylor Arms—1920 / Printed by
Frederick Reynolds
Aquatint Series #18
Blind stamp: ELC and CMC
Gift of Eliza Lefferts and Charles Montague
Cooke, Jr., 1927 (6516)

The Butterfly, 1920
Fletcher 48; Arms 47
Etching, aquatint printed on medium-weight
wove paper
10¹⁄₄ x 7³⁄₈ in. (26.0 x 18.7 cm)
6/75; second state; printed by Frederick
Reynolds
Signed, dated, and inscribed l.r. margin: John
Taylor Arms—1920 / Printed by Frederick
Reynolds; titled l.l. margin: The Butterfly.
Aquatint Series #18
Gift of Richard H. and Helen T. Hagemeyer,
1993 (24,031)

Isola Bella, Lake Maggiore, 1920
Also called *Island in Lake Maggiore, Isola Bella*
Fletcher 49; Arms 48
Etching, aquatint printed in color on heavyweight
Japanese wove paper
5¹⁵⁄₁₆ x 13⁵⁄₈ in. (15.1 x 34.6 cm)
Artist's proof; second state; printed by
Frederick Reynolds
Signed, dated, and inscribed l.r. margin:
John Taylor Arms—1920 / Printed by
Frederick Reynolds—
Aquatint Series #19
Purchase, C. Montague Cooke, Jr. Fund, 1993
(24,078)

Wasps, 1920
Also called *Aircraft Patrol* and *In Search*
Fletcher 51; Arms 50

Etching, aquatint printed in blue ink on
heavyweight card stock
7⁷⁄₈ x 5¹⁄₂ in. (20.0 x 14.0 cm)
Artist's proof; printed by Frederick Reynolds
Signed, dated, and inscribed l.r. margin:
John Taylor Arms—1920 / Printed by
Frederick Reynolds
Aquatint Series #21
Gift of Richard H. and Helen T. Hagemeyer,
1989 (20,614)

A Swordfisherman, Nantucket, 1920
Also called *Nantucket Schooner* and
A Sword Fisherman
Fletcher 52; Arms 51
Etching, aquatint printed on medium-weight
laid paper
3¹⁵⁄₁₆ x 3 in. (10.0 x 7.6 cm)
1/75; second state; printed by Frederick
Reynolds
Signed, dated, and inscribed l.r. margin:
John Taylor Arms—1920 / Printed by
Frederick Reynolds; inscribed l.l. margin: A.
Aquatint Series #22
Blind stamp: ELC and CMC
Gift of Eliza Lefferts and Charles Montague
Cooke, Jr., 1927 (6521)

Dawn, Lake Como, 1920
Also called *Dawn*
Fletcher 53; Arms 52
Etching, aquatint printed on medium-weight
laid paper
7¹⁄₄ x 5¹⁄₈ in. (18.4 x 13.0 cm)
7/75; second state; printed by Frederick
Reynolds
Signed, dated, and inscribed l.r. margin:
John Taylor Arms—1920 / Printed by
Frederick Reynolds
Aquatint Series #23
Blind stamp: ELC and CMC
Gift of Eliza Lefferts and Charles Montague
Cooke, Jr., 1927 (6518)

An Old Courtyard, Italy, 1920
Also called *Italian Courtyard*
Fletcher 54; Arms 53
Etching, aquatint printed on medium-weight
laid paper
7⁷⁄₁₆ x 6³⁄₄ in. (18.9 x 17.1 cm)
17/75; second state
Signed and dated l.r. margin: John Taylor
Arms—1920.
Aquatint Series #24
Gift of Richard H. and Helen T. Hagemeyer,
1989 (20,615)

The Sarah Jane, New York, 1920
Also called *The Sarah Jane*
Fletcher 56; Arms 58
Etching printed on medium-weight wove paper
10⁵⁄₁₆ x 7¹⁄₄ in. (26.2 x 18.4 cm)
48/78; first state
Signed and dated l.r. margin: John Taylor
Arms—1920—
Aquatint Series #26; New York Series #6
Gift of Lila L. and James F. Morgan, 1983
(18,568)

The Sarah Jane, New York, 1920
Also called *The Sarah Jane*
Fletcher 56; Arms 58

Etching, aquatint printed on medium-weight
laid paper
10³⁄₈ x 7³⁄₈ in. (26.4 x 18.7 cm)
20/50; second state; printed by Frederick
Reynolds
Signed, dated, and inscribed l.r. margin:
John Taylor Arms—1920 / Printed by
Frederick Reynolds; New York Series #6
Aquatint Series #26; New York Series #6
Blind stamp: ELC and CMC
Gift of Eliza Lefferts and Charles Montague
Cooke, Jr., 1927 (6520)

Merry Xmas from Dorothy and John Arms, 1920,
1920
Fletcher 57; Arms 59
Etching, aquatint printed in green ink on
medium-weight laid paper
5¹⁄₂ x 4¹⁄₄ in. (14.0 x 10.8 cm)
Trial proof; second state; printed by Frederick
Reynolds
Signed, dated, and inscribed l.r. margin:
John Taylor Arms—1920 / Printed by
Frederick Reynolds; signed with initials
l.l. margin: J.T.A.; inscribed in plate: TO
HAPPINESS—1921 / —MERRY XMAS— /
DOROTHY & JOHN ARMS
Aquatint Series #27; Christmas Card Series #5
Gift of Richard H. and Helen T. Hagemeyer,
1993 (24,032)

Road to the Pasture, Somewhere in Maine, 1920
Also called *Road to the Pasture* and
Le Chemin du Pâturage
Fletcher 58; Arms 60
Etching printed on medium-weight laid paper
8¹⁄₂ x 4¹¹⁄₁₆ in. (21.6 x 11.9 cm)
Trial proof; printed by Frederick Reynolds
Signed, dated, and inscribed l.r. margin:
John Taylor Arms—1920 / Printed by
Frederick Reynolds
Maine Series #2
Blind stamp: ELC and CMC
Gift of Eliza Lefferts and Charles Montague
Cooke, Jr., 1927 (6527)

Road to the Pasture, Somewhere in Maine, 1920
Also called *Road to the Pasture* and
Le Chemin du Pâturage
Fletcher 58; Arms 60
Etching printed on medium-weight laid paper
8¹⁄₂ x 4¹¹⁄₁₆ in. (21.6 x 11.9 cm)
Signed l.r. margin: John Taylor Arms—; titled
l.l. margin: Le chemin du páturage [sic]
Maine Series #2
Gift of Richard H. and Helen T. Hagemeyer,
1989 (20,616)

A Maine Home, 1920
Also called *Returning Home* and *Home Coming*
and *La Maison à Maine*
Fletcher 59; Arms 61
Etching printed on lightweight antique laid paper
5¹⁄₄ x 8¹⁄₈ in. (13.3 x 20.6 cm)
Artist's proof
Signed and dated l.r. margin: John Taylor Arms
1920; signed with initials l.l. plate: J.T.A.;
initialed l.r. margin: J.T.A.
Maine Series #3
Gift of Richard H. and Helen T. Hagemeyer,
1989 (20,617)

A Maine Home, 1920
Also called *Returning Home* and *Home Coming*
and *La Maison à Maine*
Fletcher 59; Arms 61
Etching printed on medium-weight laid paper
5⁵⁄₁₆ x 8¼ in. (13.5 x 21.0 cm)
Signed and dated l.r. margin: John Taylor
Arms—1920; signed with initials l.l. plate: J.T.A.
Maine Series #3
Gift of Richard H. and Helen T. Hagemeyer,
1992 (23,846)

The Trapper's Home, 1920
Also called *Work is Never Done* and
La Maison du Trappeur
Fletcher 60; Arms 62
Etching printed on medium-weight laid paper
5¹¹⁄₁₆ x 8¹³⁄₁₆ in. (14.4 x 22.4 cm)
4/75
Signed and dated l.r. margin: John Taylor
Arms—1920—
Maine Series #4
Gift of Richard H. and Helen T. Hagemeyer,
1988 (20,483)

The Trapper's Home, 1920
Also called *Work is Never Done* and
La Maison du Trappeur
Fletcher 60; Arms 62
Etching printed on medium-weight laid paper
5¾ x 8¹³⁄₁₆ in. (14.6 x 22.4 cm)
5/75; printed by Frederick Reynolds
Signed, dated, and inscribed l.r. margin:
John Taylor Arms—1920 / Printed by
Frederick Reynolds
Maine Series #4
Blind stamp: ELC and CMC
Gift of Eliza Lefferts and Charles Montague
Cooke, Jr., 1927 (6526)

The Old Exe Bridge, 1920
Also called *Exe Bridge* and *Vieux Pont à Exeter*
Fletcher 61; Arms 63
Etching printed on medium-weight Japanese
laid paper
4⁵⁄₈ x 6³⁄₈ in. (11.8 x 16.2 cm)
5/100
Signed and dated l.r. margin: John Taylor
Arms—1920.
Maine Series #5
Gift of Richard H. and Helen T. Hagemeyer,
1989 (20,618)

The Cabin in the Woods, 1920
Also called *The Cabin in Maine* and
La Maison Petite à Maine
Fletcher 62; Arms 64
Etching printed on medium-weight laid paper
5 x 6¹⁵⁄₁₆ in. (12.7 x 17.6 cm)
19/75
Signed and dated l.r. margin: John Taylor
Arms—1920—
Maine Series #6
Gift of Richard H. and Helen T. Hagemeyer,
1989 (20,619)

Tangled Birch, Maine, 1920
Also called *Tangled Birch* and
Les Branches Entre-Lacées
Fletcher 63; Arms 65
Etching printed on medium-weight laid paper
5⁷⁄₈ x 4 in. (14.9 x 10.2 cm)
17/75

Signed and dated l.r. margin: John Taylor
Arms—1920—
Maine Series #7
Gift of Richard H. and Helen T. Hagemeyer,
1989 (20,620)

The Inlet, Rangeley, 1920
Also called *La Voie, Rangeley*
Fletcher 64; Arms 66
Etching printed on medium-weight laid paper
3 x 5 in. (7.6 x 12.7 cm)
6/50
Signed and dated l.r. margin: John Taylor
Arms—1920
Maine Series #8
Gift of Richard H. and Helen T. Hagemeyer,
1989 (20,621)

Moonlight, Rangeley Lake, 1920
Also called *Clair de Lune, Rangeley*
Fletcher 65; Arms 67
Mezzotint printed in green ink on medium-
weight laid paper
7¹⁵⁄₁₆ x 4⁷⁄₈ in. (20.2 x 12.4 cm)
Signed and dated l.r. margin: John Taylor
Arms—1920
Maine Series #9
Purchase, C. Montague Cooke, Jr. Fund, 1993
(24,079)

The Haunted Camp, 1920
Also called *The Deserted Camp* and
Le Camp Abandonné
Fletcher 66; Arms 68
Etching printed on medium-weight laid paper
7¹⁵⁄₁₆ x 9⁷⁄₈ in. (20.2 x 25.1 cm)
11/75
Signed and dated l.r. margin: John Taylor
Arms—1920—
Maine Series #10
Gift of Richard H. and Helen T. Hagemeyer,
1991 (21,155)

Apple Tree, 1920
Also called *The Blighted Tree, Fairfield* and
La Pommier
Fletcher 67; Arms 69
Etching printed on medium-weight laid paper
7¹⁄₁₆ x 7⁷⁄₈ in. (17.9 x 20.0 cm)
Trial proof; printed by Frederick Reynolds
Signed, dated, and inscribed l.r. margin: John
Taylor Arms—1920 / Printed by Frederick
Reynolds; inscribed l.l. margin: Ed-75 Price-12⁰⁰
Gift of Richard H. and Helen T. Hagemeyer,
1989 (20,622)

Trout Pool, 1920
Also called *Fisherman's Delight* and
L'Étang des Truites
Fletcher 70; Arms 72
Etching printed on medium-weight laid paper
7 x 5 in. (17.8 x 12.7 cm)
Signed l.r. margin: John Taylor Arms; titled and
inscribed l.l. margin: L'étang des truites / 120-
Maine Series #13
Gift of Richard H. and Helen T. Hagemeyer,
1989 (20,623)

"John's Place," 1920
Also called *Chez Jean*
Fletcher 71; Arms 73
Etching printed on medium-weight laid paper
3 x 4¹⁵⁄₁₆ in. (7.6 x 12.5 cm)

Trial proof; printed by Frederick Reynolds
Signed, dated, and inscribed l.r. margin: John
Taylor Arms—1920 / Printed by Frederick
Reynolds; inscribed l.l. margin: Ed-65 Price-8⁰⁰
Maine Series #14
Gift of Richard H. and Helen T. Hagemeyer,
1989 (20,624)

"Pete" and "Topsy," 1920
Fletcher 72; Arms 74
Etching printed on medium-weight laid paper
5⁹⁄₁₆ x 6³⁄₈ in. (14.1 x 16.2 cm)
21/65
Signed and dated l.r. margin: John Taylor
Arms—1920—; signed with initials and dated l.l.
plate: J.T.A. '20
Maine Series #15
Gift of Richard H. and Helen T. Hagemeyer,
1989 (20,625)

Bridge, Rangeley Inlet, 1920
Also called *Inlet Bridge, Fishing, Rangeley Lake*
and *Le Pont à Rangeley*
Fletcher 73; Arms 75
Etching printed on medium-weight laid paper
4 x 6⁷⁄₁₆ in. (10.2 x 16.4 cm)
Signed l.r. margin: John Taylor Arms
Maine Series #16
Gift of Richard H. and Helen T. Hagemeyer,
1989 (20,626)

The White Ladies, 1920
Also called *The Three Graces*
Fletcher 74; Arms 76
Etching printed on medium-weight laid paper
7⁷⁄₁₆ x 3¹⁵⁄₁₆ in. (18.9 x 10.0 cm)
4/75
Signed and dated l.r. margin: John Taylor
Arms—1920
Maine Series #17
Gift of Richard H. and Helen T. Hagemeyer,
1989 (20,627)

The Log Bridge, 1920
Also called *The Wooden Bridge* and
La Parit de Billes
Fletcher 81; Arms 83
Etching printed on medium-weight laid paper
5⁷⁄₈ x 7¹⁵⁄₁₆ in. (14.9 x 20.2 cm)
Signed l.r. margin: John Taylor Arms—
Maine Series #24
Gift of Richard H. and Helen T. Hagemeyer,
1989 (20,628)

Farmhouse Door, 1920
Also called *Farmer's Doorway, "The Mrs."* and
La Porte du Fermier
Fletcher 84; Arms 86
Etching printed on medium-weight laid paper
5¹⁵⁄₁₆ x 3¹⁵⁄₁₆ in. (15.1 x 10.0 cm)
Signed l.r. margin: John Taylor Arms
Maine Series #27
Gift of Richard H. and Helen T. Hagemeyer,
1989 (20,629)

Evening, Kennebago Stream, 1920
Also called *Kennebago, Evening* and
La Crépuscule sur le Ruisseau
Fletcher 87; Arms 89
Etching printed on medium-weight laid paper
3 x 5½ in. (7.6 x 14.0 cm)
4/50
Signed and dated l.r. margin: John Taylor
Arms—1920

Maine Series #30
Gift of Richard H. and Helen T. Hagemeyer,
1989 (20,630)

Beaver House, 1920
Also called *Au Nord*
Fletcher 88; Arms 90
Etching printed on medium-weight laid paper
5¹⁵/₁₆ x 7⁷/₈ in. (15.1 x 20.0 cm)
10/75
Signed and dated l.r. margin: John Taylor
Arms—1920—; titled and inscribed l.l.margin:
Beaver House—12
Maine Series #31
Gift of Richard H. and Helen T. Hagemeyer,
1989 (20,631)

Loop-the-Loop, 1920
Also called *Acrobat*
Fletcher 89; Arms 91
Etching, aquatint printed on medium-weight
Japanese wove paper
5⁷/₈ x 3¹⁵/₁₆ in. (14.9 x 10.0 cm)
Artist's proof
Signed l.r. margin: John Taylor Arms—
Aquatint Series #28
Gift of Richard H. and Helen T. Hagemeyer,
1993 (25,100)

A Gargoyle, Lincoln Cathedral, 1920
Fletcher 92; Arms 94
Etching printed on medium-weight wove paper
1⁷/₈ x 3¹/₈ in. (4.8 x 7.9 cm)
Signed l.r. margin: John Taylor Arms—
Gargoyle Series #2; Miniature Series #5
Gift of Richard H. and Helen T. Hagemeyer,
1989 (20,632)

Cobwebs, 1921
Also called *Brooklyn Bridge*
Fletcher 95; Arms 97
Etching printed on medium-weight laid paper
9⁵/₈ x 7¹/₂ in. (24.4 x 19.1 cm)
Signed l.r. margin: John Taylor Arms.
New York Series #7
Purchase, Academy Volunteers Fund, 1993
(24,094)

Patterns, 1921
Also called *Mrs. Field's Demonstration*
Fletcher 96; Arms 98
Etching printed on medium-weight laid paper
6 x 4¹¹/₁₆ in. (15.2 x 11.9 cm)
Signed with initials l.l. plate: J.T.A.; inscribed
l.l. plate: Demonstration Plate / etched in forty
minutes / before Mrs Fields Club / Thurs.,
Jan 6, 1921.
Demonstration Series #3
Gift of Richard H. and Helen T. Hagemeyer,
1989 (20,633)

Memories, 1921
Also called *Rembrandt Club Demonstration*
Fletcher 97; Arms 99
Etching printed on medium-weight wove paper
5¹⁵/₁₆ x 4³/₄ in. (15.1 x 12.1 cm)
Signed and dated l.r. margin: John Taylor Arms
1921; inscribed and dated u.l. plate:
Demonstration Plate / etchet [sic] before
Rembrandt Club—40 mins. / February 7, 1921
Demonstration Series #4
Gift of Richard H. and Helen T. Hagemeyer,
1991 (21,156)

Watching the People Below, Amiens Cathedral,
1921
Also called *Amiens Cathedral*
Fletcher 101; Arms 103
Etching printed on medium-weight laid paper
5 x 8¹/₈ in. (12.7 x 20.6 cm)
20/75
Signed and dated l.r. margin: John Taylor
Arms—1921.
Gargoyle Series #3
Blind stamp: ELC and CMC
Gift of Eliza Lefferts and Charles Montague
Cooke, Jr., 1927 (6524)

Guardians of the Spire, 1921
Also called *Amiens Cathedral Number Two* and
Gardiens de la Flèche, Amiens
Fletcher 102; Arms 104
Etching printed on medium-weight laid paper
6⁵/₈ x 9⁷/₈ in. (16.8 x 25.1 cm)
7/75
Signed and dated l.r. margin: John Taylor
Arms—1921.
Gargoyle Series #4
Gift of Lila L. and James F. Morgan, 1983
(18,567)

An American Cathedral, 1921
Also called *The Woolworth Building*
Fletcher 107; Arms 109
Etching printed in brown ink on medium-weight
laid paper
17¹/₄ x 6¹³/₁₆ in. (43.8 x 17.3 cm)
Signed l.r. margin: John Taylor Arms—
New York Series #10
Gift of Richard H. and Helen T. Hagemeyer,
1989 (20,634)

A Roof in Thiers, 1921
Also called *An Ancient Roof* and
Un Toit à Thiers
Fletcher 115; Arms 117
Etching printed on medium-weight green
laid paper
6³/₈ x 3¹/₈ in. (16.2 x 7.9 cm)
Signed and dated l.r. margin: John Taylor
Arms—1921
Gift of Richard H. and Helen T. Hagemeyer,
1989 (20,635)

A Doorway in Thiers, 1921
Also called *Thiers, Ancient Portal* and *Thiers,
Nourisson Librairie Papeterie*
Fletcher 117; Arms 119
Etching printed on medium-weight wove paper
4¹/₈ x 2¹/₄ in. (10.5 x 5.7 cm)
Signed l.r. margin: John Taylor Arms.
Miniature Series #9
Gift of Richard H. and Helen T. Hagemeyer,
1991 (21,157)

The Twins, 1922
Also called *Ancient Gables, The Twins
(Imprimerie et Lithographie)*
Fletcher 119; Arms 121
Etching printed on medium-weight laid paper
10⁵/₈ x 5¹⁵/₁₆ in. (27.0 x 15.1 cm)
Signed l.r. margin: John Taylor Arms
Gable Series #8
Gift of Richard H. and Helen T. Hagemeyer,
1991 (21,158)

Our Studio Door, 1922
Also called *La Porte de Mon Atelier*
Fletcher 125; Arms 127
Etching printed on medium-weight laid paper
5¹/₈ x 3³/₄ in. (13.0 x 9.5 cm)
Signed l.r. margin: John Taylor Arms; signed l.l.
plate: J.T. ARMS
Christmas Card Series #7
Purchase, C. Montague Cooke, Jr. Fund, 1993
(24,080)

The Gates of the City, 1922
Also called *Brooklyn Bridge, Gates of New York*
Fletcher 126; Arms 128
Etching, aquatint printed in color on medium-
weight laid paper
8⁷/₈ x 8¹/₂ in. (22.5 x 21.6 cm)
Signed l.r. margin: John Taylor Arms
Aquatint Series #38; New York Series #13
Purchase, C. Montague Cooke, Jr. Fund, 1987
(19,947)

The Red Mill, 1922
Also called *The Red Barn, Southport*
Fletcher 127; Arms 130
Etching printed in brown ink on medium-
weight laid paper
11¹/₈ x 7⁵/₁₆ in. (28.3 x 18.6 cm)
First state
Signed l.r. margin: John Taylor Arms.
Aquatint Series #39
Gift of Richard H. and Helen T. Hagemeyer,
1989 (20,637)

Brig "Oleander," 1923
Fletcher 131; Arms 134
Etching, aquatint printed in color on
heavyweight wove paper
8⁵/₈ x 10¹/₈ in. (21.9 x 25.7 cm)
Second state
Signed and dated l.r. margin: John Taylor
Arms—1923; inscribed l.l. margin: Private
collection "e;" stamped in black ink l.l. margin:
COLLECTION-E / JOHN TAYLOR ARMS
Note: from the collection of the artist
Aquatint Series #41; Sailing Ship Series #5
Gift of Richard H. and Helen T. Hagemeyer,
1990 (20,816)

Le Penseur de Notre Dame, 1923
Fletcher 136; Arms 139
Etching printed on medium-weight Japanese
wove paper
12⁵/₈ x 10¹/₈ in. (32.1 x 25.7 cm)
First state
Signed and dated l.r. margin: John Taylor
Arms—1923; titled and inscribed l.l margin:
Le Penseur de Notre Dame (No 11 of the
"Gargoyle Series"
Gargoyle Series #11
Gift of Walter Crandall, 1970 (16,185)

The "Adam," 1923
Also called *La Maison Adam* and *Café Adam*
Fletcher 138; Arms 140
Etching printed on medium-weight laid paper
5³/₄ x 3¹⁵/₁₆ in. (14.6 x 10.0 cm)
Signed and dated l.r. margin: John Taylor
Arms—1923; signed and dated l.l. plate:
Arms / 1923
Gift of Richard H. and Helen T. Hagemeyer,
1990 (20,817)

Bellevue, 1923
Graphite on medium-weight coated card stock
Image: 5⅞ x 3¹⁵⁄₁₆ in. (14.9 x 10.0 cm);
sheet: 10⅝ x 7½ in. (27.0 x 19.1 cm)
Titled and dated l.r. image: BELLEVUE.
OCT. 30—
Note: preliminary drawing for *The "Adam"*
(F.138)
Gift of Richard H. and Helen T. Hagemeyer,
1988 (20,480)

*Merry Christmas from Dorothy and
John Taylor Arms*, 1923
Also called *Meudon*
Fletcher 139; Arms 141
Etching printed on heavyweight wove paper
3¼ x 4¾ in. (8.3 x 12.1 cm)
Signed with initials l.r. plate: J.T.A; inscribed
and dated l.c. plate: MERRY CHRISTMAS /
FROM / DOROTHY & JOHN TAYLOR
ARMS / MEUDON—1923
Christmas Card Series #8
Gift of Richard H. and Helen T. Hagemeyer,
1990 (20,818)

Burgos, 1924
Also called *A Spanish Town Revisited*
Fletcher 142; Arms 144
Etching printed on medium-weight Japanese
wove paper
8⅝ x 13¹⁄₁₆ in. (21.9 x 33.2 cm)
Signed and dated l.r. margin: John Taylor
Arms—1924
Spanish Church Series #2
Gift of Richard H. and Helen T. Hagemeyer,
1988 (20,485)

"La Giralda," Seville, 1924
Also called *Seville IVRS*
Fletcher 145; Arms 147
Etching printed on medium-weight Japanese
wove paper
12⁵⁄₁₆ x 7¾ in. (31.3 x 19.7 cm)
Printed by Frederick Reynolds
Signed and dated l.r. margin: John Taylor
Arms—1924; titled, inscribed, and signed
with initials l.l. margin: "La Giralda", Seville /
Number 4 of the "Spanish Churches" / First
and only state. / Clear, transparent impression,
printed on Yeddokami paper (unsized Japanese
vellum) by Frederick Reynolds in New York.—
J.T.A.; inscribed l.r. margin: In effort to suggest
the delicate, lacelike character of the architecture
and the warm, luminous / quality of the light
in pure outline, with a minimum of shading
and stipple.
Spanish Church Series #4
Gift of Richard H. and Helen T. Hagemeyer,
1990 (20,819)

Angoulême, 1924
Also called *Byzantine Revisited, Angoulême* and
The Cathedral of St. Pierre
Fletcher 146; Arms 148
Etching printed on medium-weight laid paper
6³⁄₁₆ x 11⁵⁄₁₆ in. (15.7 x 28.7 cm)
Signed and dated l.r. margin: John Taylor
Arms—1924; signed and dated l.l. plate:
ARMS 1924; titled and inscribed l.l. margin:
Angouleme / 175
French Church Series #2
Gift of Richard H. and Helen T. Hagemeyer,
1990 (20,820)

Dorothy & John Taylor Arms, Christmas 1924,
1924
Also called *Gerona*
Fletcher 147; Arms 149
Etching printed on lightweight wove paper
6¼ x 2⁷⁄₁₆ in. (15.9 x 6.2 cm)
First state
Signed l.r. margin: John Taylor Arms; titled
lower plate: • DOROTHY • & • / • JOHN •
TAYLOR • ARMS • / • CHRISTMAS • 1924
•; inscribed u.l. plate: GERONA
Christmas Card Series #9
Gift of Richard H. and Helen T. Hagemeyer,
1990 (20,821)

Nassau Hall, 1925
Also called *Princeton: Nassau Hall*
Fletcher 153; Arms 155
Etching printed on medium-weight laid paper
6⅞ x 4⁷⁄₁₆ in. (17.5 x 11.3 cm)
Artist's proof
Signed l.r. margin: John Taylor Arms—
Princeton Series #1
Gift of Richard H. and Helen T. Hagemeyer,
1990 (20,822)

Blair Arch, Princeton, 1925
Fletcher 154; Arms 156
Etching printed on medium-weight laid paper
4⅜ x 6¹¹⁄₁₆ in. (11.1 x 17.0 cm)
Trial proof #2
Signed with initials l.r. margin: J.T.A.
Princeton Series #2
Gift of Richard H. and Helen T. Hagemeyer,
1993 (25,101)

Cleveland Tower, Graduate College, Princeton,
1925
Fletcher 155; Arms 157
Etching printed on medium-weight laid paper
6¹³⁄₁₆ x 4½ in. (17.3 x 11.4 cm)
Signed l.r. margin: John Taylor Arms—
Princeton Series #3
Gift of Richard H. and Helen T. Hagemeyer,
1993 (25,102)

'79, Princeton, 1925
Fletcher 157; Arms 159
Etching printed on medium-weight laid paper
6¹³⁄₁₆ x 4½ in. (17.3 x 11.4 cm)
Trial proof #4
Signed l.r. margin: John Taylor Arms
Princeton Series #5
Gift of Richard H. and Helen T. Hagemeyer,
1990 (20,823)

Rouen, 1925
Also called *The Cathedral of Notre Dame,
From the South*
Fletcher 162; Arms 164
Etching printed on medium-weight laid paper
8⁵⁄₁₆ x 8⅛ in. (21.1 x 20.6 cm)
Signed and dated l.r. margin: John Taylor
Arms—1925
French Church Series #4
Gift of Richard H. and Helen T. Hagemeyer,
1990 (20,824)

Old Corner, Rouen, 1925
Also called *Rouen, An Old Corner* and
Un Vieux Coin à Rouen
Fletcher 163; Arms 165
Etching printed on heavyweight wove paper
6⅛ x 4 in. (15.6 x 10.2 cm)

Signed l.r. margin: John Taylor Arms
Note: Kerr Eby assisted Arms with this plate
Gift of Richard H. and Helen T. Hagemeyer,
1990 (20,825)

Abbeville, 1925
Also called *St. Vulfran*
Fletcher 165; Arms 167
Etching printed on medium-weight laid paper
7½ x 7¹³⁄₁₆ in. (19.1 x 19.8 cm)
Signed and dated l.r. margin: John Taylor
Arms—1925
French Church Series #5
Gift of Richard H. and Helen T. Hagemeyer,
1990 (20,826)

Bourges, 1925
Also called *The Cathedral of St. Étienne*
Fletcher 166; Arms 168
Etching printed on medium-weight laid paper
14⅛ x 9⅛ in. (35.9 x 23.2 cm)
Signed and dated l.r. margin: John Taylor
Arms—1925
French Church Series #6
Gift of Richard H. and Helen T. Hagemeyer,
1990 (20,827)

Fiesole, 1925
Also called *An Ancient Tower, Fiesole* and
Fiesole: The Campanile and *Fiesole (Italie)*
Fletcher 169; Arms 171
Etching printed on medium-weight laid paper
8 x 5¹⁄₁₆ in. (20.3 x 12.9 cm)
Signed and dated l.r. margin: John Taylor
Arms—1925
Note: Kerr Eby assisted Arms with this plate
Italian Series #3
Gift of Richard H. and Helen T. Hagemeyer,
1990 (20,828)

La Chiesa, Borgio, 1926
Fletcher 178; Arms 180
Etching printed on medium-weight antique
green-gray laid paper
6³⁄₁₆ x 4½ in. (15.7 x 11.4 cm)
Signed and dated l.r. margin: John Taylor
Arms—1926—; signed and dated l.r. plate:
Arms—1926
Italian Series #7
Gift of Richard H. and Helen T. Hagemeyer,
1990 (20,829)

Street in Borgio, 1926
Fletcher 179; Arms 181
Etching printed on medium-weight laid paper
3½ x 1¹¹⁄₁₆ in. (8.9 x 4.3 cm)
Signed and dated l.r. margin: John Taylor
Arms—1926; signed and dated l.r. plate:
Arms '26
Miniature Series #12
Gift of Richard H. and Helen T. Hagemeyer,
1990 (20,830)

A Pisan Court, 1926
Fletcher 180; Arms 182
Etching printed on medium-weight antique
green-gray laid paper
8¾ x 6¼ in. (22.2 x 15.9 cm)
Signed and dated l.r. margin: John Taylor
Arms—1926—; signed and dated l.r. plate:
Arms 1926
Italian Series #8
Gift of Richard H. and Helen T. Hagemeyer,
1990 (20,831)

Amiens, 1926
Also called *The Cathedral of Notre Dame,
From the Lower Town*
Fletcher 181; Arms 183
Etching printed on medium-weight laid paper
10¾ x 9⅞ in. (27.3 x 25.1 cm)
Signed and dated l.r. margin: John Taylor
Arms—1926—; signed and dated l.l. plate:
ARMS 1926
French Church Series #8
Gift of Richard H. and Helen T. Hagemeyer,
1990 (20,832)

Mont Saint-Michel, 1926
Also called *Abbey Church of St.-Michel*
Fletcher 182; Arms 184
Etching printed on medium-weight laid paper
15³⁄₁₆ x 11¹¹⁄₁₆ in. (38.6 x 29.7 cm)
Artist's proof; printed by David Strang
Signed and dated l.r. margin: John Taylor
Arms 1926; signed and dated l.r. plate: J.T.
ARMS—1926
French Church Series #9
Gift of Walter Crandall, 1970 (16,192)

*Chapiteau Gothique, Dorothy et John Taylor
Arms, A.D. MCMXXVI*, 1926
Also called *Gothic Capital*
Fletcher 185; Arms 187A
Etching printed on lightweight antique
green-gray laid paper
5¼ x 3¹¹⁄₁₆ in. (13.3 x 9.4 cm)
Second state
Signed and dated l.r. margin: John Taylor
Arms—1926
Miniature Series #14
Gift of Richard H. and Helen T. Hagemeyer,
1988 (20,486)

Rocamadour, 1927
Fletcher 186; Arms 188
Etching printed on medium-weight laid paper
13¹³⁄₁₆ x 10¹⁄₁₆ in. (35.1 x 25.6 cm)
Trial proof #3; first state
Signed and dated l.r. margin: John Taylor
Arms—1927—; titled and dated l.r. plate:
ROCAMADOUR 1926; inscribed l.l. margin:
Trial proof[III] First State / One of two
French Church Series #10
Gift of Edith G. Manuel, 1943 (12,013)

Rocamadour, 1927
Fletcher 186; Arms 188
Etching printed on lightweight Japanese
laid paper
13¹³⁄₁₆ x 9¹¹⁄₁₆ in. (35.1 x 24.6 cm)
Second state
Signed and dated l.r. margin: John Taylor
Arms—1927; titled and dated l.r. plate:
ROCAMADOUR 1926
French Church Series #10
Gift of Richard H. and Helen T. Hagemeyer,
1990 (20,833)

Église de Notre Dame, Bourg-en-Bresse, 1927
Also called *Bourg*
Fletcher 187; Arms 189
Etching printed on medium-weight antique
laid paper
8¾ x 4⅛ in. (22.2 x 10.5 cm)
Signed and dated l.c. margin: John Taylor
Arms—1927; signed and dated l.r. plate:
Arms 1926; titled upper plate: Eglise de Brou

French Church Series #11
Gift of Richard H. and Helen T. Hagemeyer,
1990 (20,834)

Venice (Sketch), 1927
Fletcher 188; Arms 190
Etching printed on medium-weight laid paper
7 x 4¹⁵⁄₁₆ in. (17.8 x 12.5 cm)
Signed and dated l.r. margin: John Taylor
Arms—1927; inscribed and dated l.c. plate:
SKETCHED, ETCHED AND PRINTED /
BEFORE THE CLUB OF ODD VOLUMES /
in 1 hr 15 mins / JAN 19 '27
Demonstration Series #17
Gift of Richard H. and Helen T. Hagemeyer,
1991 (21,159)

Rodez, 1927
Also called *The Tower of Notre Dame*
Fletcher 189; Arms 191
Etching printed on lightweight Japanese
laid paper
11⅞ x 4¹⁵⁄₁₆ in. (30.2 x 12.5 cm)
Signed and dated l.r. margin: John Taylor
Arms—1927—; signed and dated l.l. plate:
ARMS—1926; titled and dated l.r. plate:
RODEZ 1926
French Church Series #12
Gift of Richard H. and Helen T. Hagemeyer,
1990 (20,835)

Albi, 1927
Also called *The Cathedral of Ste. Cécile*
Fletcher 190; Arms 192
Etching printed on medium-weight laid paper
9⁹⁄₁₆ x 10⅛ in. (24.3 x 25.7 cm)
Signed and dated l.r. margin: John Taylor
Arms—1927; signed and dated l.l. plate:
Arms 1926; titled and dated l.r. plate: —
ALBI—1926—
French Church Series #13
Gift of Richard H. and Helen T. Hagemeyer,
1990 (20,836)

Il Sacro Monte, Varese, 1927
Also called *Varese*
Fletcher 191; Arms 193
Etching printed on lightweight antique
green-gray laid paper
7¹⁵⁄₁₆ x 7¼ in. (20.2 x 18.4 cm)
Signed and dated l.r. margin: John Taylor
Arms—1927.; titled and dated l.c. plate:
SACRO MONTE, VARESE—'26
Italian Series #9
Gift of Richard H. and Helen T. Hagemeyer,
1990 (20,837)

"La Mangia," Siena, 1927
Also called *La Torre del Mangia, Siena*
Fletcher 192; Arms 194
Etching printed on medium-weight laid paper
15¹⁄₁₆ x 8 in. (38.3 x 20.3 cm)
Signed and dated l.r. margin: John Taylor
Arms—1927; signed and dated l.l. plate:
ARMS 1927; titled lower plate: LA TORRE
DEL MANGIA, SIENA
Italian Series #10
Gift of Richard H. and Helen T. Hagemeyer,
1990 (20,838)

Chartres, 1927
Also called *Cathedral of Notre Dame from the
River* and *Notre Dame de Chartres*

Fletcher 193; Arms 195
Etching printed on lightweight antique
laid paper
13¼ x 9¹⁵⁄₁₆ in. (33.7 x 25.2 cm)
Second state
Signed and dated l.c. margin: John Taylor
Arms—1928; signed, titled, and dated l.l. plate:
J.T. ARMS / CHARTRES 1924
French Church Series #14
Purchase, 1934 (10,278)

Via Facchini, Pisa, 1927
Fletcher 194; Arms 196
Etching printed on lightweight antique green
laid paper
11¼ x 5⁷⁄₁₆ in. (28.6 x 13.8 cm)
Signed and dated l.r. margin: John Taylor
Arms—1927; titled l.l. plate: VIA /
FACCHINI ["N" in reverse] / PISA
Italian Series #11
Gift of Richard H. and Helen T. Hagemeyer,
1990 (20,839)

Saint Bénigne, Dijon, 1927
Also called *The Cathedral of St. Bénigne, Dijon*
Fletcher 195; Arms 197
Etching printed on lightweight Japanese
laid paper
10⁷⁄₁₆ x 6¹³⁄₁₆ in. (26.5 x 17.3 cm)
Artist's proof; printed by Frederick Reynolds
Signed and dated l.r. margin: John Taylor
Arms—1927; titled and dated l.l. plate: SAINT
BÉNIGNE, DIJON 1924
French Church Series #15
Gift of Richard H. and Helen T. Hagemeyer,
1990 (20,840)

Coutances, 1927
Also called *Notre Dame and St. Pierre*
Fletcher 197; Arms 199
Etching printed on lightweight antique
green-gray laid paper
9⅜ x 4¹³⁄₁₆ in. (23.8 x 12.2 cm)
Signed and dated l.r. margin: John Taylor
Arms—1927; titled and dated l.r. plate:
COUTANCES 1926
French Church Series #16
Gift of Richard H. and Helen T. Hagemeyer,
1990 (20,841)

Église Saint Michel, Pont L'Évêque, 1927
Also called *Pont L'Évêque, Church of St. Michael*
Fletcher 198; Arms 200
Etching printed on lightweight antique
green-gray laid paper
9¼ x 4¹⁵⁄₁₆ in. (23.5 x 12.5 cm)
Signed and dated l.r. margin: John Taylor
Arms—1927; titled l.l. plate: Eglise St. Michel,
Pont l'Eveque
French Church Series #17
Gift of Richard H. and Helen T. Hagemeyer,
1988 (20,484)

A Saint, Chartres, 1927
Also called *A Caryatid of Chartres Cathedral*
Fletcher 199; Arms 201
Etching printed on medium-weight blue
laid paper
5³⁄₁₆ x 1¹⁄₁₆ in. (13.2 x 2.7 cm)
Titled upper and lower plate: A Saint / Chartres
Christmas Card Series #12; Miniature Series #15
Gift of Richard H. and Helen T. Hagemeyer,
1988 (20,487)

Saint Paul, Alpes Maritimes, 1927
Fletcher 201; Arms 203
Etching printed on lightweight Japanese
laid paper
7⁹/₁₆ x 11⁹/₁₆ in. (19.2 x 29.4 cm)
Signed and dated l.r. margin: John Taylor
Arms—1927; titled, signed, and dated l.r. plate:
St Paul, Alpes Maritimes— / Arms 1927
Gift of Richard H. and Helen T. Hagemeyer,
1993 (25,103)

Château Stockalper, Brique, 1927
Fletcher 202; Arms 204
Etching printed on lightweight laid paper
10³/₁₆ x 4⁷/₈ in. (25.9 x 12.4 cm)
Signed and dated l.r. margin: John Taylor
Arms—1927
Gift of Richard H. and Helen T. Hagemeyer,
1990 (20,842)

Old Rouen, 1927
Fletcher 203; Arms 205
Etching printed on medium-weight laid paper
6⁷/₈ x 3¹³/₁₆ in. (17.5 x 9.7 cm)
Signed and dated lower margin: John Taylor
Arms—1927; titled l.r. plate: OLD Rouen
Gift of Richard H. and Helen T. Hagemeyer,
1991 (21,160)

Street in Blois (Sketch), 1927
Fletcher 204; Arms 206
Etching printed on medium-weight laid paper
6¹⁵/₁₆ x 5 in. (17.6 x 12.7 cm)
Titled l.l. plate: STREET IN BLOIS
Demonstration Series #18
Gift of Richard H. and Helen T. Hagemeyer,
1990 (20,843)

Le Pont Notre Dame, Mende, 1927
Also called *The Cathedral of Notre Dame, Seen
from the Pont Notre Dame*
Fletcher 205; Arms 207
Etching printed on medium-weight laid paper
8 x 12½ in. (20.3 x 31.7 cm)
Signed and dated l.r. margin: John Taylor
Arms—1927—
French Church Series #19
Gift of Richard H. and Helen T. Hagemeyer,
1990 (20,844)

Cathédrale de Saint Julien, Le Mans, 1927
Also called *Le Mans, The Cathedral and
Old Town*
Fletcher 206; Arms 208
Etching printed on medium-weight Japanese
wove paper
9³/₁₆ x 9¹¹/₁₆ in. (23.3 x 24.6 cm)
Signed and dated l.r. margin: John Taylor
Arms—1927—; inscribed and dated l.l. plate:
LE MANS—1926
French Church Series #20
Gift of Richard H. and Helen T. Hagemeyer,
1990 (20,845)

Street in Porto Maurizio, 1927
Fletcher 207; Arms 209
Etching printed on lightweight Japanese
laid paper
9⁹/₁₆ x 4³/₁₆ in. (24.3 x 10.6 cm)
Artist's proof
Signed and dated l.r. margin: John Taylor
Arms—1928; titled l.l. plate: STREET IN
PORTO MAURIZIO; initialed l.r. margin: JTA
Italian Series #13

Gift of Richard H. and Helen T. Hagemeyer,
1991 (21,161)

A Tower of Saint Front, Périgueux, 1928
Also called *Périgueux's Tower of Saint Front*
Fletcher 212; Arms 214
Etching printed on lightweight antique
laid paper
12 x 5⁹/₁₆ in. (30.5 x 14.1 cm)
Artist's proof
Signed and dated l.r. margin: John Taylor
Arms—1928; signed and dated l.l. plate:
ARMS 1928—; initialed l.r. margin: J.T.A.
French Church Series #22
Gift of Richard H. and Helen T. Hagemeyer,
1991 (21,162)

Le Puy, 1928
Also called *The Cathedral of Notre Dame and the
Chapel of St. Michael*
Fletcher 214; Arms 216
Etching printed on medium-weight laid paper
9³/₄ x 13¹/₁₆ in. (24.8 x 33.2 cm)
Trial proof #1; second state
Signed and dated l.r. margin: John Taylor
Arms—1928; signed and dated l.r. plate: —
ARMS 1928
French Church Series #23
Gift of Richard H. and Helen T. Hagemeyer,
1991 (21,163)

Saint Germain L'Auxerrois, Paris, 1928
Also called *St. Germain L'Auxerre*
Fletcher 215; Arms 217
Etching printed on medium-weight laid paper
9⁷/₈ x 5 in. (25.1 x 12.7 cm)
Personal proof
Signed and dated l.r. margin: John Taylor
Arms—1928; signed and dated l.l. plate:
ARMS, 1928; titled l.r. plate: SAINT
GERMAIN L'AUXERROIS
French Church Series #24
Gift of Richard H. and Helen T. Hagemeyer,
1990 (20,846)

Saint Germain L'Auxerrois, Paris, 1928
Also called *St. Germain L'Auxerre*
Fletcher 215; Arms 217
Etching printed on medium-weight laid paper
9⁷/₈ x 5 in. (25.1 x 12.7 cm)
Signed and dated l.r. margin: John Taylor
Arms—1928; signed and dated l.l. plate:
ARMS, 1928; titled l.r. plate: SAINT
GERMAIN L'AUXERROIS
French Church Series #24
Blind stamps: ELC and CMC; CHICAGO /
SOCIETY / OF / ETCHERS [in circle with
etching press]
Gift of Eliza Lefferts and Charles Montague
Cooke, Jr., 1947 (12,344)

From the Tower, Bayeux, 1928
Fletcher 216; Arms 218
Etching printed on lightweight Japanese
wove paper
5³/₈ x 2¹⁵/₁₆ in. (13.7 x 7.5 cm)
Signed and dated l.c. margin: John Taylor
Arms—1928; signed and dated l.l. plate:
ARMS '28
Note: mounted on Christmas card
Christmas Card Series #13
Gift of Richard H. and Helen T. Hagemeyer,
1990 (20,847)

Lescure, Une Tour des Remparts, 1928
Fletcher 217; Arms 219
Etching printed on medium-weight laid paper
6⁷/₁₆ x 3¹⁵/₁₆ in. (16.4 x 10.0 cm)
Signed and dated l.l. margin: John Taylor
Arms—1928; signed and dated l.l. plate:
J.T. ARMS 1928
Gift of Richard H. and Helen T. Hagemeyer,
1990 (20,848)

Basilica of the Madeleine, Vézelay, 1929
Also called *The Abbey Church of Ste. Madeleine*
Fletcher 223; Arms 225
Etching printed on medium-weight antique
green-gray laid paper
12³/₄ x 7³/₈ in. (32.4 x 18.7 cm)
Third state
Signed and dated l.r. margin: John Taylor
Arms—1929; titled l.c. margin: ABBEY
CHURCH OF STE. MADELEINE VEZELAY;
signed and dated l.l. plate: J.T. ARMS / 1929
French Church Series #28
Purchase, 1934 (10,279)

*Abside de la Cathédrale de Saint Pierre et Saint
Paul, Troyes*, 1929
Also called *Apse of the Cathedral of Saints Peter
and Paul, Troyes*
Fletcher 224; Arms 226
Etching printed on medium-weight antique
green-gray laid paper
12⁵/₈ x 5³/₈ in. (32.1 x 13.7 cm)
Signed and dated l.r. margin: John Taylor
Arms—1930; signed and dated l.l. plate: John T.
Arms—1929; inscribed l.l. margin: Edition 100
French Church Series #29
Gift of Richard H. and Helen T. Hagemeyer,
1990 (20,849)

Rio del Santi Apostoli, 1930
Fletcher 226; Arms 228
Etching printed on medium-weight antique
green-gray laid paper
8¹/₁₆ x 6¹/₈ in. (20.5 x 15.6 cm)
Trial proof; first state
Signed with initials and dated l.r. margin:
J.T.A—1930; inscribed l.l. margin: Only proof
of First State of the plate—
Italian Series #14
Gift of Richard H. and Helen T. Hagemeyer,
1988 (20,488)

The Enchanted Doorway, Venezia, 1930
Also called *La Porta della Carta, Venezia* and
Venezia '29
Fletcher 227; Arms 229
Etching printed on medium-weight antique
laid paper
12⁵/₈ x 6⁵/₈ in. (32.1 x 16.8 cm)
Artist's proof; printed by Henry E. Carling
Signed and dated l.r. margin: John Taylor
Arms—1930; signed, titled, and dated
l.r. plate: —J.T. ARMS— / VENEZIA '29
Italian Series #15
Gift of Richard H. and Helen T. Hagemeyer,
1990 (20,850)

Shadows of Venice, 1930
Also called *Il Ponte di Rialto, Venezia*
Fletcher 229; Arms 231
Etching, aquatint printed on lightweight
blue-gray laid paper
10¹/₄ x 12¹/₈ in. (26.0 x 30.8 cm)
Second state

Signed and dated l.r. margin: John Taylor Arms—1930; signed, inscribed, and dated l.r. plate: JT ARMS / VENEZIA 1929; inscribed l.l. margin: Edition 100
Italian Series #16
Gift of Richard H. and Helen T. Hagemeyer, 1990 (20,851)

Porta del Paradiso, Venezia, 1930
Fletcher 230; Arms 232
Etching printed on lightweight antique laid paper
7½ x 3¹³/₁₆ in. (19.1 x 9.7 cm)
Signed and dated l.r. margin: John Taylor Arms—1930; titled l.c. margin: Porta del Paradiso.; signed, inscribed, and dated l.l. plate: J.T. ARMS / VENEZIA—1929; inscribed, signed, and dated l.l. margin: To Mrs. F.L. Griggs / with sincerest best wishes / John Taylor Arms—1930
Italian Series #17
Gift of Richard H. and Helen T. Hagemeyer, 1990 (20,852)

La Bella Venezia, 1930
Also called *The Grand Canal, Venice*
Fletcher 232; Arms 234
Etching printed in brown ink on lightweight antique laid paper
7¼ x 16½ in. (18.4 x 41.9 cm)
Signed and dated l.r. margin: John Taylor Arms—1931; signed, inscribed, and dated l.r. plate: John Taylor Arms / Venezia 1930; inscribed l.l. margin: Private collection "f;" inscribed, signed, and dated l.l. margin: To my very dear friend Frank G. Kennedy Jr. / John Taylor Arms—1931—
Note: from F.G. Kennedy collection, New York
Italian Series #18
Gift of Richard H. and Helen T. Hagemeyer, 1990 (20,853)

Venetian Filigree, 1931
Also called *Ca' d'Oro Venetia*
Fletcher 235; Arms 237
Etching printed on medium-weight laid paper
10¾ x 11 in. (27.3 x 27.9 cm)
Signature stamped in ink l.r. margin: John Taylor Arms.
Italian Series #20
Gift of James Jensen and Jennifer Saville in honor of Richard H. and Helen T. Hagemeyer, 1993 (24,081)

The Piazza, Venzone, 1931
Fletcher 239; Arms 241
Etching printed on lightweight antique laid paper
5⅛ x 7⅜ in. (13.0 x 18.7 cm)
Signed and dated l.r. margin: John Taylor Arms—1931; inscribed l.l. margin: Ed 100
Italian Series #23
Gift of Richard H. and Helen T. Hagemeyer, 1990 (20,854)

Chinon (Sketch), 1931
Fletcher 242; Arms 244
Etching printed on heavyweight wove paper
5⅞ x 3¹⁵/₁₆ in. (14.9 x 10.0 cm)
Inscribed and signed lower margin: Demonstration Plate, etched before the college club of Bridgeport, Nov. 4, 1931 / John Taylor Arms—
Demonstration Series #27
Gift of Richard H. and Helen T. Hagemeyer, 1990 (20,855)

Canale e Chiesa, San Barnaba, Venezia (Sketch), 1931
Fletcher 243; Arms 245
Etching printed on heavyweight wove paper
6⅞ x 4⅞ in. (17.5 x 12.4 cm)
Inscribed and signed lower margin: Demonstration Plate, etched at the National Arts club, Wednesday, December 9, 1931 / John Taylor Arms—; titled l.c. plate: CANALE E CHIESA SAN BARNABA
Demonstration Series #28
Gift of Richard H. and Helen T. Hagemeyer, 1991 (21,164)

La Tour d'Horloge, Dinan, 1932
Fletcher 246; Arms 248
Etching printed on lightweight antique green laid paper
9⅜ x 4 in. (23.8 x 10.2 cm)
Second state
Signed and dated l.r. margin: John Taylor Arms—1932; inscribed l.l. margin: Ed 100ᴵᴵ
French Church Series #33
Gift of Richard H. and Helen T. Hagemeyer, 1988 (20,489)

A Breton Calvary, 1932
Also called *Calvaire du Seizième Siècle*
Fletcher 247; Arms 249
Etching printed on heavyweight wove paper
5⁹/₁₆ x 3⅛ in. (14.1 x 7.9 cm)
Second state
Signed and dated l.r. margin: John Taylor Arms—1932; titled lower plate: • Calvaire • du • Seizième • Siècle •; inscribed l.l. margin: Ed 75ᴵᴵ
Miniature Series #16
Gift of Richard H. and Helen T. Hagemeyer, 1990 (20,856)

Saint Catherine's Belfry, Honfleur, 1932
Fletcher 248; Arms 250
Etching printed on medium-weight laid paper
13⅝ x 7¹/₁₆ in. (34.6 x 17.9 cm)
Second state
Signed and dated in ink l.r. margin: John Taylor Arms—1932; titled in ink l.l. margin: St. Catherine's Belfry, Honfleur; inscribed, signed, and dated in ink l.l. margin: To G. Alan Chidsay, with my compliments / John Taylor Arms. 1938
French Church Series #34
Gift of Richard H. and Helen T. Hagemeyer, 1990 (20,857)

Église Saint Gervais, Gisors, 1932
Fletcher 249; Arms 251
Etching printed on medium-weight wove paper
10⅛ x 8⁷/₁₆ in. (25.7 x 21.4 cm)
Artist's proof; printed by David Strang
Signed and dated l.r. margin: John Taylor Arms—1932; titled l.l. margin: Église St. Gervais, Gisors
French Church Series #35
Gift of Richard H. and Helen T. Hagemeyer, 1990 (20,858)

Towers of San Gimignano, 1932
Also called *Stern Towers*
Fletcher 250; Arms 252
Etching, aquatint printed on lightweight antique laid paper
10⅞ x 7¼ in. (27.6 x 18.4 cm)

Second state
Signed and dated l.r. margin: John Taylor Arms—1932; inscribed l.l. margin: Ed 100ᴵᴵ
Italian Series #24
Gift of Richard H. and Helen T. Hagemeyer, 1990 (20,859)

San Marino (Sketch), 1933
Fletcher 255; Arms 257
Etching printed on medium-weight laid paper
6¹⁵/₁₆ x 4¹⁵/₁₆ in. (17.6 x 12.5 cm)
First state
Signed and dated l.r. margin: John Taylor Arms—1933; inscribed l.l. margin: To my friend Fritz Ray Carrington—Saluti! / Demonstration plate, etched at University [indecipherable], January 14, 1933; inscribed and signed with initials lower margin: Hardly a "Six's Bridge", but much earnest effort went into it and the time was short! / J.T.A.
Demonstration Series #32
Gift of Richard H. and Helen T. Hagemeyer, 1991 (21,165)

Study in Stone, Cathedral of Orense, 1933
Fletcher 257; Arms 259
Etching printed on medium-weight laid paper
7⅜ x 5⁹/₁₆ in. (18.7 x 14.1 cm)
Second state; printed by David Strang
Signed and dated l.r. margin: John Taylor Arms—1933; inscribed l.l. margin: Ed 100ᴵᴵ
Spanish Church Series #8
Purchase, 1934 (10,277)

Study in Stone, Cathedral of Orense, 1933
Fletcher 257; Arms 259
Etching printed on medium-weight laid paper
7⅜ x 5⁹/₁₆ in. (18.7 x 14.1 cm)
Second state; printed by David Strang
Signed and dated l.r. margin: John Taylor Arms—1933; inscribed l.l. margin: Ed 100ᴵᴵ
Spanish Church Series #8
Gift of Mr. and Mrs. Lester G. Will, 1976 (16,697)

San Francesco nel Deserto (Sketch), 1933
Fletcher 261; Arms 264
Etching printed on medium-weight laid paper
4⅞ x 6⅞ in. (12.4 x 17.5 cm)
Proof
Titled, inscribed, and signed lower margin: "Sketch, San Francesco nel Deserto." With the compliments of the artist. Proof from Demonstration Plate / drawn, etched, and printed in 2 hours at the residence of Mrs Henry F. Noyes, Pinehurst, N.C., Feb 13, 1933 / John Taylor Arms
Demonstration Series #38
Gift of Richard H. and Helen T. Hagemeyer, 1990 (20,860)

Puerta del Obispo, Zamora, 1933
Also called *The Bishop's Door, Zamora*
Fletcher 266; Arms 270
Etching printed on medium-weight antique laid paper
12⅝ x 7¼ in. (32.1 x 18.4 cm)
Second state
Signed and dated l.r. margin: John Taylor Arms—1933; inscribed l.l. margin: Ed 100ᴵᴵ
Spanish Church Series #9
Gift of Richard H. and Helen T. Hagemeyer, 1990 (20,861)

Stone Tapestry, San Isidoro, León, 1933
Also called *South Portal of the Collegiate Church of San Isidor, León*
Fletcher 267; Arms 271
Etching printed on medium-weight laid paper
11⅝ x 3¹/₁₆ in. (29.5 x 7.8 cm)
Trial proof 12; printed by David Strang
Signed and dated l.r. margin: John Taylor Arms—1933; signed with initials l.l. plate: J.TA.; inscribed lower plate: Collegialis ecclesiae & / Leonensis regi Isidoro / sancto dedicatae meri- / diano de latere exscri- / pta est baec imago & / Anno Domini MCXLIX
Spanish Church Series #10
Gift of Richard H. and Helen T. Hagemeyer, 1990 (20,862)

Stone Tapestry, San Isidoro, León, 1933
Also called *South Portal of the Collegiate Church of San Isidor, Léon*
Fletcher 267; Arms 271
Etching printed on medium-weight laid paper
11⅝ x 3¹/₁₆ in. (29.5 x 7.8 cm)
Signed and dated l.r. margin: John Taylor Arms—1933; titled and inscribed l.l. margin: Stone Tapestry / Detail of the South Portal of the Collegiate Church of San Isidoro, Leon. / Number 10 of the "Spanish Churches;" signed with initials l.l. plate: J.TA.; inscribed l.l. margin: Ed. 100ᴵ; inscribed lower plate: Collegialis ecclesiae & / Leonensis regi Isidoro / sancto dedicatae meri- / diano de latere exscri- / pta est baec imago & / Anno Domini MCXLIX
Spanish Church Series #10
Gift of John Taylor Arms, 1935 (10,390)

Mediaeval Pageantry, 1933
Fletcher 270B; Arms 274
Etching printed on medium-weight laid paper
12¾ x 8¾ in. (32.4 x 22.2 cm)
Fourth state
Signed l.r. margin: Kerr Eby imp. / John Taylor Arms—; inscribed l.l. margin: Ed 100ᴵⱽ
Note: this plate was the work of both Arms and Eby. Arms etched the buildings; Eby did the figures and trees. Both artists signed all prints other than first state proofs; those prints designated for Eby carry his signature first.
French Church Series #36
Gift of Richard H. and Helen T. Hagemeyer, 1990 (20,863)

The Valley of the Savery, Wyoming, 1934
Also called *Savery, Wyoming*
Fletcher 276; Arms 280
Etching printed on lightweight green-gray laid paper
7¹³/₁₆ x 14³/₁₆ in. (19.8 x 36.0 cm)
Third state
Signed and dated l.r. margin: John Taylor Arms—1934; titled l.l. plate: VALLEY OF THE SAVERY; inscribed l.l. margin: Ed 100ᴵᴵᴵ
Gift of Richard H. and Helen T. Hagemeyer, 1990 (20,864)

The Valley of the Savery, Wyoming, 1934
Graphite on lightweight wove paper
Image: 7⅞ x 14³/₁₆ in. (20.0 x 36.0 cm); sheet: 8⅞ x 15 in. (22.5 x 38.1 cm)
Signed with initials and dated l.r. margin: J.T.A.—1934; inscribed l.l. margin: Private collection "a"
Note: preliminary drawing for *The Valley of the Savery* (F.276); from the Dorothy Noyes Arms collection

Gift of Richard H. and Helen T. Hagemeyer, 1988 (20,479)

Puerta Principal de la Iglesia de San Pablo, Valladolid, 1934
Also called *Miniature, San Pablo, Valladolid*
Fletcher 278; Arms 282
Etching printed on medium-weight green-gray antique laid paper
4⅞ x 3¹⁵/₁₆ in. (12.4 x 10.0 cm)
Second state
Signed and dated l.r. margin: John Taylor Arms—1934; signed l.r. plate: John Taylor Arms; titled lower plate: Puerta Principal de la Iglesia • de San Pablo • / • Valladolid •; inscribed l.l. margin: Ed 100ᴵᴵ
Spanish Church Series #11
Gift of Richard H. and Helen T. Hagemeyer, 1993 (25,104)

"La Colegiata," Toro, 1935
Fletcher 284; Arms 288
Etching printed on medium-weight laid paper
9¾ x 12¾ in. (24.8 x 32.4 cm)
Trial proof #2; second state; printed by Charles S. White
Signed and dated l.r. margin: John Taylor Arms—1935
Spanish Church Series #12
Gift of Richard H. and Helen T. Hagemeyer, 1990 (20,865)

Santa Maria Major, Ronda, 1935
Fletcher 288; Arms 292
Etching printed on medium-weight laid paper
8 x 5⅜ in. (20.3 x 13.7 cm)
Signed and dated l.r. margin: John Taylor Arms—1935
Spanish Church Series #13
Gift of Richard H. and Helen T. Hagemeyer, 1991 (21,171)

Notre Dame the Tiny, 1935
Also called *The West Facade of Notre Dame, Paris* and *West Facade of Notre Dame Cathedral*
Fletcher 290; Arms 294
Etching printed on lightweight laid paper
Image: 1½ x ⅞ in. (3.8 x 2.3 cm); platemark: 6¹⁵/₁₆ x 4¹⁵/₁₆ in. (17.6 x 12.5 cm)
Signed and dated below l.r. image: John Taylor Arms 1935; signed and dated l.r. margin: John Taylor Arms 1935; titled below l.l. image: Notre Dame the Tiny—; titled lower plate: Notre Dame the Tiny
Christmas Card Series #17; Miniature Series #18; French Church Series #37; Brooch Series #1
Gift of Eliza Lefferts and Charles Montague Cooke, Jr., 1939 (11,140)

From Knoedler's Window, MCMXXXV, 1935
Fletcher 293B; Arms 297
Etching printed on medium-weight laid paper
5⅛ x 4¹⁵/₁₆ in. (13.0 x 12.5 cm)
Artist's proof; fourth state; printed by David Strang
Signed and dated l.r. margin: John Taylor Arms 1935; titled lower plate: From Knoedler's Window MCMXXXV; inscribed, signed, and dated l.l. margin: To Margaret Howard Ramey [?] / with my compliments / John Taylor Arms, 1941
New York Series #14
Gift of Richard H. and Helen T. Hagemeyer, 1990 (20,866)

Rouen (Sketch), 1935
Fletcher 294; Arms 298
Etching printed on medium-weight laid paper
6¹⁵/₁₆ x 4¹⁵/₁₆ in. (17.6 x 12.5 cm)
Signed and dated l.r. margin: John Taylor Arms 1935; titled and inscribed lower margin: Sketch, Rouen—Demonstration plate etched at the Slater Memorial Museum, Norwich, Conn., December 9, 1935; inscribed l.l. margin: Private collection "b"
Note: from Margery Arms Roberts collection
Demonstration Series #62
Gift of Richard H. and Helen T. Hagemeyer, 1990 (20,867)

Honfleur (Sketch), 1936
Fletcher 300; Arms 304
Etching printed on medium-weight laid paper
6¾ x 4¹³/₁₆ in. (17.1 x 12.2 cm)
Titled, inscribed, and signed lower margin: Sketch, Honfleur—Demonstration Plate etched for the students of the School of The / National Academy of Design, NYC, on the afternoons of March 2nd, 11th, and 16th 1936 / John Taylor Arms
Demonstration Series #68
Gift of Richard H. and Helen T. Hagemeyer, 1988 (20,490)

Crystal and Jade, 1936–40
Also called *Homage to Jacquemart*
Fletcher 301; Arms 305
Etching, aquatint printed on lightweight green laid paper
7½ x 6¹¹/₁₆ in. (19.1 x 17.0 cm)
Sixth state
Signed and dated l.r. margin: John Taylor Arms 1940
Purchase, C. Montague Cooke, Jr. Fund, 1993 (24,082)

Louviers Lace, 1936
Also called *Porte du Baptême, Église Notre Dame, Louviers*
Fletcher 303; Arms 307
Etching printed on heavyweight wove paper
13¹³/₁₆ x 9¹¹/₁₆ in. (35.1 x 24.6 cm)
Third state
Signed and dated l.r. margin: John Taylor Arms 1936; inscribed l.l. margin: Ed 100ᴵᴵᴵ
French Church Series #38
Gift of Richard H. and Helen T. Hagemeyer, 1990 (20,868)

Oviedo, The Holy, 1937
Fletcher 306; Arms 311
Etching printed on medium-weight laid paper
12¼ x 4⁷/₁₆ in. (31.1 x 11.3 cm)
Third state
Signed and dated l.r. margin: John Taylor Arms 1937; inscribed l.l. margin: Ed. 109ᴵᴵᴵ
Spanish Church Series #14
Gift of Richard H. and Helen T. Hagemeyer, 1990 (20,869)

Gloria: Saint Riquier, 1937
Also called *The Church of Saint Riquier* and *Gloria Ecclesiae Antiquae*
Fletcher 307; Arms 312
Etching printed on medium-weight wove paper
12¾ x 8⅝ in. (32.4 x 21.9 cm)
Fourth state
Signed and dated l.r. margin: John Taylor

Arms—1937; titled l.l. margin: Gloria Ecclesiae Antiquae / (Church of St. Riquier, France); inscribed, signed, and dated l.l. margin: To my friend Norman Kent / John Taylor Arms—1938
French Church Series #39
Gift of Richard H. and Helen T. Hagemeyer, 1990 (20,870)

Anglia Antiqua, West Walton, 1937
Also called *The Church of West Walton*
Fletcher 310; Arms 315
Etching printed on medium-weight laid paper
5⁷/₁₆ x 2¹⁵/₁₆ in. (13.8 x 7.5 cm)
Signed and dated l.c. margin: John Taylor Arms 1937; signed and dated l.r. plate: John Taylor Arms—1937
English Series #1; Miniature Series #20
Purchase, 1937 (10,885)

Reflections at Finchingfield, England, 1938
Fletcher 311; Arms 316
Etching printed on medium-weight laid paper
7¹/₈ x 17³/₁₆ in. (18.1 x 43.7 cm)
Artist's proof; second state; printed by David Strang
Signed and dated l.r. margin: John Taylor Arms—1938; titled, inscribed, and signed with initials l.l. margin: Reflections at Finchingfield / Finchingfield is a small, little known village in Essex, not far from Saffron Waldron and Thaxted. / I tumbled upon it by chance in the course of an English pilgrimage in 1936— J.T.A.; signed and dated l.r. plate: John Taylor Arms—1937; inscribed, signed, and dated l.l. margin: To Walter B. Crandall, with sincerest good wishes / John Taylor Arms, 1938
English series #2
Gift of Walter Crandall, 1970 (16,195)

In Memoriam, 1939
Also called *The North Portal of Chartres Cathedral*
Fletcher 317; Arms 322
Etching printed on medium-weight laid paper
14⁵/₈ x 12 in. (37.2 x 30.5 cm)
Artist's proof; second state; printed by David Strang
Signed and dated l.r. margin: John Taylor Arms—1939
French Church Series #40
Purchase, 1941 (11,811)

Lavenham, England, 1939
Fletcher 322; Arms 327
Etching printed on medium-weight green-gray laid paper
7³/₈ x 3⁷/₈ in. (18.7 x 9.8 cm)
Third state
Signed and dated l.r. margin: John Taylor Arms 1939
English Series #4
Gift of Richard H. and Helen T. Hagemeyer, 1990 (20,871)

Lavenham, England, 1939
Fletcher 322; Arms 327
Etching printed on medium-weight laid paper
7³/₈ x 3⁷/₈ in. (18.7 x 9.8 cm)
Third state
Signed and dated l.r. margin: John Taylor Arms 1939
English Series #4

Gift of Richard H. and Helen T. Hagemeyer, 1991 (21,166)

Lavenham, England, 1939
Fletcher 322; Arms 327
Etching printed on medium-weight laid paper
7⁷/₁₆ x 3⁷/₈ in. (18.9 x 9.8 cm)
Third state
Signed and dated l.r. margin: John Taylor Arms 1939
English Series #4
Gift of Edith G. Manuel, 1943 (12,014)

Stanwick Churchyard, 1939
Fletcher 324; Arms 332
Etching printed on medium-weight green laid paper
2³/₈ x 3⁵/₁₆ in. (6.0 x 8.4 cm)
Artist's proof; fourth state; printed by David Strang
Signed and dated l.r. margin: John Taylor Arms 1939; titled l.l. margin: Stanwick Churchyard; inscribed, signed, and dated l.l. margin: To my friend Norman Kent / John Taylor Arms 1939
English Series #6; Miniature Series #22
Gift of Richard H. and Helen T. Hagemeyer, 1991 (21,168)

Ledbury, England (Sketch), 1939
Fletcher 328; Arms 333
Etching printed on medium-weight laid paper
5⁷/₈ x 4 in. (14.9 x 10.2 cm)
Proof
Titled, inscribed, signed, and dated lower margin: Sketch, Ledbury—Proof from Demonstration Plate drawn, / etched, and printed, in two hours at Wesleyan University. / November 10, 1939. To Marian B. Munson / with the compliments of the artist / John Taylor Arms—1939
Demonstration Series #83
Gift of Richard H. and Helen T. Hagemeyer, 1990 (20,872)

Aspiration, La Madeleine, Verneuil-sur-Avre, 1939
Also called *Fraternité, Egalité, Liberté*
Fletcher 329; Arms 334
Etching printed on medium-weight laid paper
15⁵/₈ x 10 in. (39.7 x 25.4 cm)
Artist's proof; fifth state; printed by David Strang
Signed and dated l.r. margin: John Taylor Arms—1939
French Church Series #41
Gift of Richard H. and Helen T. Hagemeyer, 1990 (20,873)

Ashwell, Hertfordshire, England (Sketch), 1940
Fletcher 332; Arms 337
Etching printed on medium-weight laid paper
5⁷/₈ x 4 in. (14.9 x 10.2 cm)
Titled, inscribed, signed, and dated lower margin: Sketch, Ashwell, Hertfordshire— Impression from Demonstra- / tion Plate drawn, etched, and printed, in two hours at the / Grand Central Art Galleries, N.Y.C., January 9, 1940 / With the compliments of the artist / John Taylor Arms 1940; titled and inscribed l.r. plate: ASHWELL—DEMONSTRATION
Demonstration Series #85
Gift of Richard H. and Helen T. Hagemeyer, 1990 (20,874)

Castello, Umbria (Sketch), 1940
Fletcher 334; Arms 339
Etching printed on heavyweight laid paper
5⁷/₈ x 3¹⁵/₁₆ in. (14.9 x 10.0 cm)
Titled, inscribed, signed, and dated lower margin: Sketch, Castello, Umbria—Impression from Demonstration Plate / drawn, etched, and printed, in two hours at the Quinnipiack Club, / New Haven, Conn., April 7, 1940 / To Mr Emerson Munson, with my compliments / John Taylor Arms 1940; titled l.l. plate: CASTELLO, UMBRIA
Demonstration Series #87
Gift of Richard H. and Helen T. Hagemeyer, 1991 (21,172)

Stranger in England, St. Lawrence, West Wycombe, Buckinghamshire, 1940
Fletcher 336; Arms 341
Etching printed on lightweight laid paper
5⁵/₈ x 2³/₄ in. (14.3 x 7.0 cm)
Third state
Signed and dated l.r. margin: John Taylor Arms 1940
English Series #8; Miniature Series #25
Gift of Richard H. and Helen T. Hagemeyer, 1991 (21,173)

Coxe Hall, Hobart College, Geneva, N.Y. (Sketch), 1940
Fletcher 337; Arms 342
Etching printed on medium-weight laid paper
3¹⁵/₁₆ x 5¹⁵/₁₆ in. (10.0 x 15.1 cm)
Artist's proof; printed by Charles S. White
Inscribed, signed, and dated lower margin: Impression from Demonstration Plate drawn, etched, and printed, in two hours at Hobart College, / Geneva, N.Y., May 9, 1940. To my friend Norman Kent, with my best wishes / John Taylor Arms—1940; titled lower plate: Coxe Hall, Administration Building, Hobart College, Geneva, New York.
Demonstration Series #88
Gift of Richard H. and Helen T. Hagemeyer, 1991 (21,174)

Shadows in Mexico (Sketch), 1940
Fletcher 340A; Arms 345
Etching printed on medium-weight laid paper
4¹⁵/₁₆ x 6⁷/₈ in. (12.5 x 17.5 cm)
Artist's proof; first state; printed by Charles S. White
Titled, inscribed, signed, and dated lower margin: Sketch, Shadows in Mexico— Impression from Demonstration Plate etched for television broadcast of "How / to Make an Etching" at studios of National Broadcasting Company, N.Y.C., July 26, 1940. / John Taylor Arms 1940
Demonstration Series #93
Gift of Richard H. and Helen T. Hagemeyer, 1991 (21,175)

Shadows in Mexico (Sketch), 1940–44
Fletcher 340B; Arms 394
Etching printed on lightweight wove paper
4⁷/₈ x 3⁷/₁₆ in. (12.4 x 8.7 cm)
Third state
Signed and dated l.r. margin: John Taylor Arms 1944
Mexican Series #1
Gift of Richard H. and Helen T. Hagemeyer, 1991 (21,177)

Chichester (Sketch), 1940
Fletcher 341; Arms 346
Etching printed on medium-weight laid paper
5⁷⁄₈ x 3¹⁵⁄₁₆ in. (14.9 x 10.0 cm)
Artist's proof; first state; printed by
Charles S. White
Titled, inscribed, and signed lower margin:
Sketch, Chichester—Impression from demon-
stration / plate drawn, etched, and printed,
in two hours at the Montclair / Art Museum,
Sept. 24, 1940.—John Taylor Arms / To Asta
from John Souvenir!
Demonstration Series #94
Gift of Richard H. and Helen T. Hagemeyer,
1991 (21,178)

Church of Saint Jean, Laigle, Orne, 1940
Fletcher 343; Arms 348
Etching printed on medium-weight laid paper
3 x 1³⁄₄ in. (7.6 x 4.4 cm)
Artist's proof; printed by David Strang
Signed and dated l.r. margin: John Taylor
Arms 1940; titled l.l. margin: Church of Saint
Jean. Laigle; inscribed, signed, and dated
l.l. margin: To my friend Norman Kent /
John Taylor Arms 1941
French Church Series #43; Miniature Series #26
Gift of Richard H. and Helen T. Hagemeyer,
1991 (21,179)

Plumed Serpent, Chichén Itzá, 1940
Fletcher 344; Arms 349
Etching printed on lightweight antique laid paper
1¹⁵⁄₁₆ x 2¹⁄₂ in. (4.9 x 6.4 cm)
Second state
Signed and dated l.r. margin: John Taylor Arms
1940
Miniature Series #27; Yucatán Series #1
Gift of James F. Jensen in memory of Joseph
Feher, 1987 (19,800)

*Holy Cross, Sarratt (and Albury), Hertfordshire
"To F.L.M.G.,"* 1940
Also called *Sarratt and Albury, Morning
"To F.L.M.G."*
Fletcher 345; Arms 350
Etching printed on medium-weight laid paper
6 x 3¹⁵⁄₁₆ in. (15.2 x 10.0 cm)
First state
Signed and dated l.r. margin: John Taylor Arms
1940; inscribed and dated l.l. plate: To F.L.M.G.
1940; inscribed lower margin: Sketch, "To
F.L.M.G." Imp. from Demonstration Plate
etched at the New England / Book Fair, Boston,
Mass. Oct 22 1940 / A "mon vieux," de J.O.A.
[?] / A little work subsequently added. Really
State II. / Souvenir d'une belle occasion!
Demonstration Series #96
Gift of Richard H. and Helen T. Hagemeyer,
1991 (21,180)

Stockholm, 1940
Fletcher 346; Arms 351
Etching, aquatint printed on medium-weight
green laid paper
7¹¹⁄₁₆ x 13⁵⁄₈ in. (19.5 x 34.6 cm)
Artist's proof; third state; printed by
Charles S. White
Signed and dated l.r. margin: John Taylor
Arms—1946
Scandinavian Series #1
Purchase, 1941 (11,812)

The Grolier Club Library (Sketch), 1941
Fletcher 353; Arms 360
Etching printed on medium-weight laid paper
3⁷⁄₈ x 5¹⁵⁄₁₆ in. (9.8 x 15.1 cm)
Signed and dated l.r. margin: John Taylor Arms
1941; titled and inscribed l.l. margin: Sketch,
Grolier Club Library. Demonstration Print.;
inscribed and signed l.l. plate: LIBRARY OF
THE GROLIER CLUB / DEMONSTRATION
PLATE, DRAWN, ETCHED, / AND PRINTED,
IN A LITTLE OVER TWO HOUR'S, / AT THE
GROLIER CLUB, NEW YORK CITY, ON /
THE EVENING OF MARCH 9, 1941 / JOHN
TAYLOR ARMS
Demonstration Series #105
Gift of Richard H. and Helen T. Hagemeyer,
1991 (21,181)

Compton Church, Surrey (Sketch), 1941
Fletcher 355; Arms 363
Etching printed on medium-weight laid paper
3¹⁵⁄₁₆ x 5¹⁵⁄₁₆ in. (10.0 x 15.1 cm)
Artist's proof, printed by Charles S. White
Titled, inscribed, signed, and dated lower
margin: Sketch, Compton Church (Surrey)—
Impression from demonstration plate drawn, /
etched, and printed, in two hours before the
Westport Women's Club, Bedford House, /
Westport, Conn., April 7, 1941 / To Mr and
Mrs Ralph Boyer, with my compliments / John
Taylor Arms 1941; titled, signed with initials,
dated, and inscribed l.l. plate: COMPTON
CHURCH, SURREY ["S" in reverse] / J.T.A.,
1941—DEM PL. 108
Demonstration Series #108
Gift of Richard H. and Helen T. Hagemeyer,
1991 (21,182)

Oxford (Sketch), 1941
Fletcher 358; Arms 366
Etching printed on medium-weight laid paper
5⁷⁄₈ x 3¹⁵⁄₁₆ in. (14.9 x 10.0 cm)
Titled, inscribed, signed, and dated lower
margin: Sketch, Oxford—Impression from
demonstration plate drawn, / etched, printed,
in two hours fifteen minutes at the Tiffany /
Foundation, Oyster Bay, L.I., NY, July 23
1941/ To my friends Mr and Mrs Hobart
Nichols / Souvenir of the occasion! / John
Taylor Arms 1941; titled, inscribed, and signed
l.c. plate: SKETCH, OXFORD, / 2 HOUR
DEMONSTRATION PLATE / ETCHED AT
TIFFANY FOUNDATION / OYSTER BAY,
L.I., JULY 23, 1941 / JOHN TAYLOR ARMS
Demonstration Series #111
Gift of Richard H. and Helen T. Hagemeyer,
1991 (21,183)

*Saint Martin's Church, Preston, Hertfordshire,
"To F.L.M.G." (Sketch)*, 1941
Fletcher 361; Arms 369
Etching printed on medium-weight laid paper
3¹⁵⁄₁₆ x 5¹⁵⁄₁₆ in. (10.0 x 15.1 cm)
Titled, inscribed, and signed lower margin:
Sketch, St. Martin's Church, Preston,
Hertfordshire / Demonstration Plate drawn,
etched, and printed at Wesleyan University,
Middletown, / Conn., October 9, 1941. With
the compliments of the artist / John Taylor
Arms.; inscribed and dated l.c. plate: DEM.
PLATE TO F.L.M.G. 1941
Demonstration Series #114
Gift of Richard H. and Helen T. Hagemeyer,
1991 (21,184)

Dreux, 1942
Fletcher 368; Arms 378
Etching printed on medium-weight laid paper
8³⁄₁₆ x 2⁷⁄₈ in. (20.8 x 7.3 cm)
Signed and dated l.r. margin: John Taylor
Arms 1942
French Church Series #44
Gift of Richard H. and Helen T. Hagemeyer,
1991 (21,185)

Stokesay Castle, 1942
Fletcher 369; Arms 379
Etching printed on medium-weight antique [?]
green laid paper
2⁵⁄₁₆ x 3¹⁄₁₆ in. (5.9 x 7.8 cm)
Second state
Signed and dated l.r. margin: John Taylor
Arms 1942
Miniature Series #30; English Series #9
Gift of Eliza Lefferts and Charles Montague
Cooke, Jr., 1943 (11,990)

Stokesay Castle, 1942
Fletcher 369; Arms 379
Etching printed on medium-weight blue laid paper
2⁵⁄₁₆ x 3 in. (5.9 x 7.6 cm)
Artist's proof; printed by David Strang
Signed and dated l.c. margin: John Taylor
Arms 1942
Miniature Series #30; English Series #9
Gift of Richard H. and Helen T. Hagemeyer,
1991 (21,186)

Corbel on Gate House, Stokesay Castle, 1944
Also called *Shropshire Corbel*
Fletcher 382; Arms 393
Etching printed on lightweight antique laid paper
3³⁄₁₆ x 1⁵⁄₈ in. (8.1 x 4.1 cm)
Second state
Signed and dated l.r. margin: John Taylor
Arms 1944
Miniature Series #32; English Series #12
Gift of Richard H. and Helen T. Hagemeyer,
1991 (21,187)

Vermont, 1944
Also called *God's Mirror*
Fletcher 384; Arms 395
Etching printed on lightweight wove paper
1⁵⁄₁₆ x 2³⁄₈ in. (3.3 x 6.0 cm)
Third state
Signed and dated l.r. margin: John Taylor Arms
1944; titled l.l. plate: GOD'S MIRROR
Christmas Card Series #22; Miniature Series #33
Gift of Walter Crandall, 1953 (13,231)

Normandy, 1944
Also called *The Church of Saint Jean Laigle, Orne*
Fletcher 385; Arms 396
Etching printed on lightweight antique laid paper
2 x 1¹⁄₄ in. (5.1 x 3.2 cm)
Third state
Signed and dated l.r. margin: John Taylor
Arms 1944
Miniature Series #34; French Church Series #45
Gift of Richard H. and Helen T. Hagemeyer,
1991 (21,188)

Light and Shade, Taxco, 1946
Fletcher 394; Arms 405
Etching printed on medium-weight laid paper
10⁷⁄₁₆ x 13¹¹⁄₁₆ in. (26.5 x 34.8 cm)
Artist's proof; second state; printed by
David Strang

Signed and dated l.r. margin: John Taylor Arms 1946; signed with monogram l.r. plate: JTA [intertwined in rectangle]
Mexican Series #2
Gift of Richard H. and Helen T. Hagemeyer, 1991 (21,189)

Greenfield Hill Congregational Church (Sketch), 1946
Fletcher 395; Arms 406
Etching printed on medium-weight laid paper
6 x 3⁷⁄₈ in. (15.2 x 9.8 cm)
Inscribed and signed lower margin: Demonstration Plate drawn, etched, printed at Fairfield High / School, March 29, 1946, for benefit of Greenfield Hill Congregational / Church. / With the compliments of the artist / John Taylor Arms; signed with monogram and dated l.l. plate: JTA / 1946 [intertwined in rectangle]; titled and inscribed l.l. plate: GREENFIELD HILL / CONGREGATIONAL CHURCH / DEMONSTRATION PLATE
Demonstration Series #135
Gift of Richard H. and Helen T. Hagemeyer, 1991 (21,190)

Nevers (Sketch), 1946
Fletcher 396; Arms 407
Etching printed on medium-weight laid paper
3⁷⁄₈ x 5¹⁵⁄₁₆ in. (9.8 x 15.1 cm)
Titled, inscribed, signed, and dated lower margin: "Sketch, Nevers"—Impression from Demonstration Plate drawn, etched, printed, in / 2¼ hrs at Wesleyan University, Middletown, Conn., May 16, 1946 / With the compliments of the artist—John Taylor Arms 1946; titled, inscribed, dated and signed with monogram u.r. plate: "SKETCH, NEVERS" DEMONSTRA-TION PLATE—WESLEYAN, 1946 ["6" in reverse] JTA [intertwined in square]
Demonstration Series #136
Gift of Richard H. and Helen T. Hagemeyer, 1991 (21,192)

Portrait of a Romanesque Capital, 1946
Also called *The Portrait of a Mediaeval Nobleman, Romanesque*
Fletcher 397; Arms 408
Etching printed on medium-weight blue laid paper
2¹¹⁄₁₆ x 2¹¹⁄₁₆ in. (6.8 x 6.8 cm)
Artist's proof; fourth state; printed by David Strang
Signed and dated l.r. margin: John Taylor Arms 1946; signed with monogram l.r. plate: JTA [intertwined in square]; inscribed l.c. plate: ROMANESQUE; monogram stamped in ink l.c. margin: JTA [intertwined]
Miniature Series #36
Gift of Richard H. and Helen T. Hagemeyer, 1988 (20,491)

"Precious Stones," 1946
Also called *Église Notre Dame—Les Andelys* and *South Transeptal Portal of the Church of Notre Dame des Andelys*
Fletcher 398; Arms 409
Etching printed on medium-weight laid paper
3¼ x 1¹⁵⁄₁₆ in. (8.3 x 4.9 cm)
Second state; printed by David Strang
Signed and dated l.r. margin: John Taylor Arms 1946; signed with monogram l.l. plate: JTA [intertwined in rectangle]; inscribed lower plate: Eglise Notre Dame / —Les Andelys; monogram stamped in ink l.c. margin: JTA [intertwined in circle]

Note: printed by David Strang for the Miniature Print Society
Miniature Series #37; French Church Series #46
Blind stamp: ELC and CMC
Gift of Eliza Lefferts and Charles Montague Cooke, Jr., 1947 (12,307)

Dinton, Buckinghamshire (Sketch), 1947
Fletcher 403; Arms 414
Etching printed on heavyweight wove paper
3¹⁵⁄₁₆ x 5¾ in. (10.0 x 14.6 cm)
Titled, inscribed, signed, and dated lower margin: Sketch, Dinton, Buckinghamshire—Demonstration Plate—2½ hrs.—Benjamin / West Society. Swarthmore, Pa.—Mar. 20 1947 / With the compliments of the artist—John Taylor Arms 1947; signed with monogram and dated l.l. plate: JTA 1947 [intertwined]; inscribed and titled l.r. plate: DEMONSTRATION ["S" in reverse] PLATE—BENJAMIN WEST ["S" in reverse] SOCIETY ["S" in reverse]—MAR 20 1947 / SKETCH, DINTON BUCKINGHAMSHIRE
Demonstration Series #141
Gift of Richard H. and Helen T. Hagemeyer, 1991 (21,193)

The Herbert Lowell Dillon Gymnasium, Princeton, N.J., 1947
Fletcher 406; Arms 417
Etching printed on medium-weight laid paper
7⁷⁄₈ x 9¼ in. (20.0 x 23.5 cm)
Artist's proof; printed by David Strang
Signed and dated l.r. margin: John Taylor Arms 1947; signed with monogram and dated l.l. plate: JTA / 45 [intertwined in square]; monogram stamped in ink l.c. margin: JTA [intertwined in a circle]; inscribed, signed, and dated l.l. margin: To my friend Malcolm Goodridge / John Taylor Arms 1948
Gift of Richard H. and Helen T. Hagemeyer, 1991 (21,194)

"Memento Vivere," Notre Dame, Évreux, 1947
Also called *The North Transept of Notre Dame Cathedral, Évreux, France*
Fletcher 407; Arms 418
Etching printed on medium-weight wove paper
13½ x 7⅛ in. (34.3 x 18.1 cm)
Second state
Signed and dated l.r. margin: John Taylor Arms 1947; signed with monogram l.c. plate (two times): JTA [intertwined]
French Church Series #47
Gift of Richard H. and Helen T. Hagemeyer, 1991 (21,195)

"Memento Vivere," Notre Dame, Évreux, 1947
Also called *The North Transept of Notre Dame Cathedral, Évreux, France*
Fletcher 407; Arms 418
Etching printed on lightweight antique laid paper
13⁹⁄₁₆ x 7⁷⁄₁₆ in. (34.5 x 17.9 cm)
Second state
Signed and dated l.r. margin: John Taylor Arms 1947; signed with monogram l.c. plate (two times): JTA [intertwined]
French Church Series #47
Gift of Eliza Lefferts Cooke in memory of Charles Montague Cooke, Jr., 1952 (13,108)

Warwick (Sketch), 1948
Also called *Leicester Hospital, Warwick, England*
Fletcher 410; Arms 421A
Etching printed on medium-weight laid paper

4 x 6 in. (10.2 x 15.2 cm)
Second state
Signed and dated l.r. margin: John Taylor Arms 1948; signed with monogram l.l. plate: JTA [intertwined]; titled and inscribed l.l. margin: "Leicester Hospital, Warwick" / Second, final state of "Sketch, Warwick," Demonstration Plate No 143
Demonstration Series #143; English Series #13
Gift of Richard H. and Helen T. Hagemeyer, 1991 (21,196)

"The Old Order," 1948
Also called *The Church of Saint Mary and "Arlington Row"* and *Bridge over Coln River at Bibury*
Fletcher 412; Arms 423
Etching printed on medium-weight laid paper
5⁵⁄₁₆ x 7⁷⁄₈ in. (13.5 x 20.0 cm)
Second state; printed by David Strang
Signed and dated l.r. margin: John Taylor Arms 1948—
English Series #14
Blind stamp: ELC and CMC
Gift of Eliza Lefferts Cooke in memory of Charles Montague Cooke, Jr., 1949 (12,578)

Espalion (Sketch), 1949
Fletcher 414; Arms 425
Etching printed on medium-weight coated wove paper
4 x 5¹⁵⁄₁₆ in. (10.2 x 15.1 cm)
Titled, inscribed, signed, and dated: "Sketch, Espalion" Impression from Demonstration Plate, drawn, etched, printed, / in 2 hrs before the Print Club of Albany, at the Albany Institute of History and / Art, Albany, NY, Mar. 3, 1949—Printed from the first and only (underbitten) state of the / plate, exactly as it was executed in the Demonstration. With the best wishes of the artist— / John Taylor Arms 1950
Demonstration Series #144
Gift of Richard H. and Helen T. Hagemeyer, 1991 (21,197)

French Lace, 1949
Also called *The West Portal of the Church of Notre Dame, Villefranche-en-Rouergue, Aveyron*
Fletcher 415; Arms 426
Etching printed on medium-weight antique green laid paper
8 x 4⅝ in. (20.3 x 11.8 cm)
Artist's proof; second state; printed by David Strang
Signed and dated l.r. margin: John Taylor Arms 1949; signed with monogram and dated l.c. plate: JTA [intertwined] / 49
French Church Series #51
Gift of Richard H. and Helen T. Hagemeyer, 1991 (21,198)

French Lace, 1949
Also called *The West Portal of the Church of Notre Dame, Villefranche-en-Rouerque, Aveyron*
Fletcher 415; Arms 426
Etching printed on medium-weight laid paper
8 x 4¹¹⁄₁₆ in. (20.3 x 11.9 cm)
Second state
Signed and dated l.r. margin: John Taylor Arms 1949; signed with monogram and dated l.c. plate: JTA [intertwined] / 49
French Church Series #51
Gift of Lila L. and James F. Morgan, 1983 (18,565)

French Lace, 1949
Also called *The West Portal of the Church of Notre Dame, Villefranche-en-Rouergue, Aveyron*
Fletcher 415; Arms 426
Etching printed on medium-weight laid paper
8 x 4¹¹⁄₁₆ in. (20.3 x 11.9 cm)
Second state
Signed and dated l.r. margin: John Taylor Arms 1949; signed with monogram and dated l.c. plate: JTA [intertwined] / 49
French Church Series #51
Blind stamp: ELC and CMC
Gift of Eliza Lefferts Cooke in memory of Charles Montague Cooke, Jr., 1949 (12,641)

"Somewhere in Warwickshire," 1949
Also called *Somewhere in England, Warwickshire*
Fletcher 417; Arms 428
Etching printed on heavyweight wove paper
4 x 6 in. (10.2 x 15.2 cm)
Titled, inscribed, and signed lower margin: "Sketch, Somewhere in Warwickshire"—Impression from Demonstration Plate drawn, / etched, printed, in 3 hrs. at a Group Demonstration of the Fine Print Media held at the National / Academy of Design, NYC, April 7, 1949—John Taylor Arms; titled, dated, and inscribed l.r. plate: SOMEWHERE IN ENGLAND / APRIL 7, 49 DEMONSTRATION OF ETCHING—N.A.D., N.YC
Demonstration Series #146
Gift of Richard H. and Helen T. Hagemeyer, 1991 (21,199)

"Spanish Profile," Palencia, 1950
Also called *La Puerta del Obispo* and *The Doorway of the Bishop, Palencia Cathedral, South Portal*
Fletcher 418; Arms 429
Etching printed on lightweight wove paper
13¹¹⁄₁₆ x 6¹³⁄₁₆ in. (34.8 x 17.3 cm)
Artist's proof; third state; printed by David Strang
Signed and dated l.r. margin: John Taylor Arms 1950; monogram stamped in ink l.r. margin: JTA [intertwined]
Spanish Church Series #15
Gift of Richard H. and Helen T. Hagemeyer, 1988 (20,492)

"Spanish Profile," Palencia, 1950
Also called *La Puerta del Obispo* and *The Doorway of the Bishop, Palencia Cathedral, South Portal*
Fletcher 418; Arms 429
Etching printed on medium-weight antique green-gray wove paper
13¾ x 6⅞ in. (34.9 x 17.5 cm)
Third state
Signed and dated l.r. margin: John Taylor Arms 1950
Spanish Church Series #15
Blind stamp: ELC and CMC
Gift of Eliza Lefferts Cooke in memory of Charles Montague Cooke, Jr., 1952 (13,084)

Church of Saint Aignan, Chartres (Sketch), 1950
Fletcher 421; Arms 432
Etching printed on lightweight antique laid paper
5¹⁵⁄₁₆ x 4 in. (15.1 x 10.2 cm)
Second state
Signed and dated l.r. margin: John Taylor Arms imp—1950; titled l.l. margin: Sketch, Saint Aignan, Chartres; inscribed and titled lower plate: DEMONSTRATION PLATE / CHURCH OF ST AIGNAN CHARTRES; signed with monogram l.l. plate: JTA [intertwined]; inscribed, signed, and dated lower margin: Demonstration Plate—Second State—Drawn, etched, printed, in 2¾ hours at / "Mill Stones", Greenfield Hill, Fairfield, Conn., Jan 13, 1950, subsequently /reworked in part. Printed on paper contemporary with the subject. / To Vicky from John, 1950; inscribed and signed with monogram l.r. margin: An exercise in speed—total time spent / on the print—drawing and etching the plate / and pulling the proof—5¼ hours / JTA [intertwined]; monogram stamped in ink l.c. margin: JTA [intertwined]
Demonstration Series #150; French Church Series #52
Gift of Richard H. and Helen T. Hagemeyer, 1991 (21,200)

Ceignac (Aveyron), 1950
Fletcher 422; Arms 433
Etching printed on heavyweight wove paper
3½ x 5⁹⁄₁₆ in. (8.9 x 14.1 cm)
Artist's proof; second state; printed by Charles S. White
Signed and dated l.r. margin: John Taylor Arms 1950; signed l.r. plate: JOHN TAYLOR ARMS; inscribed, signed, and dated l.l. margin: To Amory from John, 1950; monogram stamped in ink l.c. margin: JTA [intertwined]
French Church Series #53
Gift of Richard H. and Helen T. Hagemeyer, 1991 (21,201)

"Black and White," Trébrivan, 1953
Also called *Trébrivan in Snow*
Fletcher 423; Arms 434
Etching, drypoint printed on heavyweight wove paper
3 x 2 in. (7.6 x 5.1 cm)
Artist's proof; third state; printed by Charles S. White
Signed and dated l.r. margin: John Taylor Arms—1953; signed with monogram l.l. plate: JTA [intertwined]
Miniature Series #41; French Church Series #54
Gift of Richard H. and Helen T. Hagemeyer, 1991 (21,203)

Cordes (Sketch), 1951
Fletcher 425; Arms 436A
Etching printed on medium-weight laid paper
6 x 3¹⁵⁄₁₆ in. (15.2 x 10.0 cm)
Second state; printed by Charles S. White

Titled, inscribed, signed, and dated lower margin: "Sketch, Cordes"—Impression from Demonstration Plate, / drawn, etched, and printed, in 2¾ hrs. at the Library of / Congress, Washington, D.C., May 22, 1951 / To Milton Kaplan, with the compliments and best / wishes of the artist.—John Taylor Arms. 1951; signed with monogram l.l. plate: JTA [intertwined]
Demonstration Series #153
Gift of Richard H. and Helen T. Hagemeyer, 1991 (21,169)

"This England" (Fairford, Gloucestershire), 1952
Also called *St. Mary Church, Fairford on the Coln*
Fletcher 426; Arms 437
Etching printed on medium-weight laid paper
6⁷⁄₁₆ x 11⁷⁄₁₆ in. (16.4 x 29.1 cm)
Artist's proof; second state; printed by Charles S. White
Signed and dated l.r. margin: John Taylor Arms 1952; signed with monogram l.l. plate: JTA [intertwined]
English Series #15
Gift of Richard H. and Helen T. Hagemeyer, 1991 (21,204)

New York Skyline, Sketch, 1921
Fletcher 435; Arms [print not recorded]
Lithograph printed on lightweight Japanese laid paper
6¾ x 5 in. (17.1 x 12.7 cm)
Printed by Bolton Brown
Signed and dated l.r. margin: John Taylor Arms—del—1921—; signed l.l. margin: Bolton Brown—imp—
Gift of Richard H. and Helen T. Hagemeyer, 1988 (20,493)

Castles in the Air, 1921
Fletcher 436; Arms [print not recorded]
Lithograph printed on lightweight Japanese laid paper
15½ x 10⅜ in. (39.4 x 26.4 cm)
Printed by Bolton Brown
Signed and dated l.r. margin: John Taylor Arms—1921; signed l.l. margin: Bolton Brown—imp—
Gift of Richard H. and Helen T. Hagemeyer, 1991 (21,205)

In Old Lisieux, 1921
Fletcher 441; Arms [print not recorded]
Lithograph printed on lightweight Japanese wove paper
9⅜ x 5 in. (23.8 x 12.7 cm)
9/27
Printed by Bolton Brown
Signed and dated l.r. margin: John Taylor Arms—1921; signed l.l. margin: Bolton Brown—imp—
Gift of Richard H. and Helen T. Hagemeyer, 1991 (21,170)

THE BIBLIOGRAPHY MAKES NO CLAIM TO BE COMPREHENSIVE. It includes material found to be informative and/or of interest to the author in the examination of Arms and his career. A listing of the primary unpublished sources precedes that of publications by Arms and his occasional collaborators and a selection of secondary sources. The first two sections are arranged chronologically; the final section is in alphabetical order, with works by the same author presented chronologically. It has not seemed useful to cite each of the articles Arms wrote as part of the series "One Hundred Masterpieces of Printmaking" published in *Print*, nor each of the introductions he contributed to the catalogues for the Society of American Etchers (and successor organizations) annual exhibitions during his thirty-three year tenure as its president, nor each review of his various exhibitions. Regarding "One Hundred Masterpieces of Printmaking," suffice it to say that the essays that comprise it appear in *Print* beginning with its first issue in 1940 and ending with the twenty-eighth in the series in 1952, about a year before Arms' death.

Unpublished Sources

Arms, John Taylor. Papers. Archives of American Art, Smithsonian Institution, Washington, D.C. On microfilm, rolls 65–69.

Arms, John Taylor and Dorothy Noyes Arms, "Descriptive Catalogue of the Work of John Taylor Arms," 2 vols., 1962 (unpublished typescript catalogue in the Prints Division of the New York Public Library, prepared from records compiled by the artist, edited by his wife, and completed after her death by his former secretaries, May Bradshaw Hays and Marie Probstfield, under the sponsorship of the New York Public Library).

Kropfl, Ulrich. "A Catalogue of the Work of John Taylor Arms, N.A., A.R.E., P.S.A.E.," 1971 (unpublished typescript catalogue in the Prints and Photographs Division of the Library of Congress, Washington, D.C.).

Publications by John Taylor Arms and Collaborators

Arms, Dorothy Noyes and John Taylor Arms. *Churches of France.* New York: The Macmillan Company, 1929.

Arms, John Taylor. "John Taylor Arms." In *John Taylor Arms,* compiled by The Crafton Collection, [1–6], vol. 5, *American Etchers.* New York: The Crafton Collection, Inc., 1930.

_____. "Among the Print Makers, Old and Modern, John Taylor Arms Reviews Academy's Print Show for Art Digest." *The Art Digest* 5, no. 5 (Dec. 1, 1930): 24–25, 3–4.

_____. "Etchings and the Brooklyn Society of Etchers." *The Brooklyn Museum Quarterly* 18, no. 2 (Apr. 1931): 57–62.

_____. "Eugene Higgins, Etcher of Life." *Prints* 1, no. 4 (May 1931): frontispiece, 1–13.

Arms, Dorothy Noyes and John Taylor Arms. *Hill Towns and Cities of Northern Italy.* New York: The Macmillan Company, 1932.

_____. "Aristocracy in Prints." *Prints* 2, no. 4 (May 1932): 28–43.

_____. "Arthur William Heintzelman, Etcher." *Prints* 3, no. 4 (May 1933): frontispiece, 1–12.

_____. "Childe Hassam, Etcher of Light." *Prints* 4, no. 1 (Nov. 1933): frontispiece, 1–12.

_____. *Handbook of Print Making and Print Makers.* New York: The Macmillan Company, 1934.

_____. "John W. Winkler, Master of Line." *Prints* 4, no. 2 (Jan. 1934): frontispiece, 1–13.

_____. "The Society of American Etchers." *Prints* 5, no. 2 (Jan. 1935): frontispiece, 1–9.

_____. "The Dry-Points of Louis Conrad Rosenberg, A.N.A." *Prints* 5, no. 4 (May 1935): 1–9.

_____. "An Exhibition That Came True." *Prints* 6, no. 5 (June 1936): 251–261.

Arms, John Taylor and Dorothy Noyes Arms. *Design in Flower Arrangement.* New York: The Macmillan Company, 1937.

Arms, John Taylor. "Self Estimate." In *Twenty-One Years of Drawing, A Retrospective Exhibition of the Work of John Taylor Arms, N.A., A.R.E., P.S.A.E.,* 6–12. exh. cat. New York: The Grand Central Art Galleries, 1937.

_____. "By-Paths in Print Collecting, French Nineteenth Century Prints—Part I." *Prints* 7, no. 4 (Apr. 1937): 194–203.

_____. "By-Paths in Print Collecting, French Nineteenth Century Prints—Part II." *Prints* 7, no. 5 (June 1937): 268–276.

_____. *Gothic Memories, Etchings and Drawings.* New York: Wm C. Popper & Co., [1938].

_____. "Ernest D. Roth, Etcher." *The Print Collector's Quarterly* 25, no. 1 (Feb. 1938): 32–57.

_____. "Prints and Print Making." *Print* 1, no. 1 (June 1940): 90–92.

_____. "John Taylor Arms Tells How He Makes an Etching, Part 1—Preparation of Plate." *American Artist* 4, no. 12 (Dec. 1940): 14–16.

_____. "John Taylor Arms Tells How He Makes an Etching, Part 2—Drawing On and Etching the Plate." *American Artist* 5, no. 1 (Jan. 1941): 10–12.

_____. "John Taylor Arms Tells How He Makes an Etching, Part 3—Printing." *American Artist* 5, no. 2 (Feb. 1941): 13–15.

Bender, J. H. and John Taylor Arms. "Perplexing Questions and Pertinent Answers." *The Print Collector's Quarterly* 28, no. 4 (Dec. 1941): 418–441.

Arms, John Taylor. "Hobart Nichols, Artist, Man, Leader: An Appraisal by John Taylor Arms." *American Artist* 7, no. 7 (Sept. 1943): 17–20.

_____. "Printmakers' Processes and a Militant Show." *Art News* 42, no. 10 (Oct. 1–14, 1943): 8–15, 32.

_____. "Credo." In *Selected Examples from Thirty Years of Etching, John Taylor Arms,* 4–9. exh. cat. New York: Kennedy & Company, 1945.

_____. "The Meaning of Prints." *The Print Collector's Quarterly* 29, no. 3 (Nov. 1948): 5–11.

Secondary Source Material

Arms, Dorothy Noyes. "John Taylor Arms, Modern Mediævalist." *The Print Collector's Quarterly* 21, no. 2 (Apr. 1934): 126–141.

_____. "Romance in the Making of Prints." In *The Romance of Fine Prints,* edited by Alfred Fowler, 10–42. Kansas City: The Print Society, 1938.

Bassham, Ben L. *John Taylor Arms, American Etcher.* exh. cat. Madison, WI: Elvehjem Art Center, University of Wisconsin-Madison, 1975.

Cary, Elizabeth Luther. "The Work of John Taylor Arms." *Prints* 1, no. 5 (Sept. 1931): 1–13.

Chamberlain, Samuel. "John Taylor Arms… Phenomenon." *Print* 1, no. 4 (Mar. 1941): 43–46.

Eaton, Cynthia. "The Aquatints of John Taylor Arms." *The Print Connoisseur* 1, no. 2 (Dec. 1920): 104–121.

_____. *John Taylor Arms, Aquatinter, An Appreciation of the Man and His Work with an Authoritative List of His Aquatints.* Boston: Charles E. Goodspeed & Co., 1923.

Fletcher, William Dolan. *John Taylor Arms, A Man for All Time, The Artist and His Work.* The Sign of the Arrow, 1982.

Heintzelman, Arthur W. "John Taylor Arms: In Memoriam." *The Boston Public Library Quarterly* 6, no. 4 (Oct. 1954): 229–234.

New York, Kennedy Galleries, Inc. *Memorial Exhibition, John Taylor Arms (1887–1953).* exh. cat. New York: Kennedy Galleries, Inc., 1954.

Morgan, Charles L. "The Pencil and John Taylor Arms." *The Print Connoisseur* 5, no. 6 (Apr. 1925): 92–125.

Pelletier, S. William. "John Taylor Arms: An American Mediaevalist." *The Georgia Review* 30, no. 4 (Winter 1976): 908–987.

_____. "John Taylor Arms: An Evaluation." *Print Review* 14 (Winter 1981): 11–25.

_____. "John Taylor Arms, His World and Work." *Georgia Museum of Art Bulletin* 17 (1993).

_____. "The Gargoyle Images of John Taylor Arms." *Print Quarterly* 7, no. 3 (Sept. 1990): 292–303.

Schaldach, William J. "John Taylor Arms, 1887–1953, An Appreciation." *Print* 8, no. 5 (Feb.–Mar. 1954): viii–ix.

Weisberg, Gabriel P. "Twentieth-Century Gothic: John Taylor Arms." *Art News* 75, no. 3 (Mar. 1976): 58–59.

Wheelock, Warren. "John Taylor Arms, Modern Mediaevalist." *Art Instruction* 3, no. 2 (Feb. 1939): 17–21, 31.

Whitmore, Elizabeth M. *John Taylor Arms, Notes on the Development of an American Etcher.* Reprinted from *The Print Connoisseur.* New York: privately printed, 1925.

Zigrosser, Carl. "John Taylor Arms." In *The Artist in America, Twenty-Four Close-Ups of Contemporary Printmakers,* 24–32. New York: Alfred A. Knopf, 1942.

Index